MW01077117

TODAY LOVES FOOD

RECIPES FROM
AMERICA'S FAVORITE KITCHEN

By the TODAY Show Family and Friends
Foreword by Ina Garten

ABRAMS, NEW YORK

"It's fun to taste the food and get new ideas to shake up what you're doing in your kitchen."

—Savannah Guthrie

THE RUNDOWN

FOREWORD
by Ina Garten

"I HOPE IT ALWAYS FEELS LIKE THIS!"

That's what I told myself on July 2, 1999, just before my first appearance on the TODAY show. The excitement, the butterflies, the glamour, the rush of it all were almost overwhelming. This was *it*; I'd made it to the big time, and it was so much fun!

But my dream was about to crash. The TODAY show had started their "Summer on the Plaza" series, and Donna Summer was on in the same hour as I was. The audience was totally psyched to see Donna Summer. The people surrounding Rockefeller Plaza were singing and dancing and having the best time.

Wait—I have to go on NEXT TO *DONNA SUMMER*??!

My husband, Jeffrey, who was watching the show on TV in a nearby hotel room, later told me that his heart sank, too. *Ina will get lost in all that energy*, he thought. And then—and he may have exaggerated just a bit—BOOM! There I was, introducing my first cookbook and showing the host my buffet of drinks and summer salads with the same energy with which Donna Summer belts out a song.

That happened because there is really nothing like the TODAY show. The extraordinary hosts make every guest, from a rock star to a nervous first-time cookbook author like me, feel totally welcomed and valued. Behind the scenes, the producers work magic by doing a staggering amount of preparation, because they want every segment to be perfect. Everyone associated with the show is brilliantly professional—and fun! And every guest benefits from their hard work.

It's not easy to produce a cooking segment for TV. For each five-minute segment to be interesting, you need to—literally—plan every second. The genius of the producers and food stylists at the TODAY show is that they capture the guest's signature cooking style in this impossibly short period of time and make the recipe seem effortless and irresistible so the audience can't wait to try it at home.

I'm so glad the TODAY show collected these great recipes in *TODAY Loves Food*. What looked so good on television will be even more delicious in your kitchen. No matter what kind of food you love to cook or eat, you'll find something here that will delight everyone at your table.

And just in case you're wondering, I've been on the TODAY show countless times since 1999, and yes, the electricity and excitement always feel like that first time.

Congratulations to the team for a brilliant cookbook!

xxxx Ina Garten

THE COLD OPEN

OUR SHOW IS A FAMILY. And what do families do? We come together and eat.

We gather around the table to connect over food—even if that means it's eight, nine, or ten in the morning and we're slamming burgers, cracking into a clambake, or sipping on a giant martini.

Since the 1950s, when TODAY was in its infancy, cooking has been an integral part of the show.

Our broadcast starts with news, which is meant to inform, and ends with food, which is meant to inspire. Our cooking segments are a welcome reprieve from turbulent headlines. We want to bring you the whole world—including what to make for dinner tonight.

In the early days, cooking segments were more formal tutorials focused on home economics and basic techniques. The draw was less about the chef and more about the lesson. But that all changed in the 1990s and early 2000s, when we saw the rise of the celebrity chef. Household names like Martha, Ina, and Bobby brought their own unique styles to cooking segments. High-end restaurant chefs ventured out of the kitchen and into our studio to share their culinary secrets.

Since then, we've also welcomed home cooks and chefs from all walks of life, who have gained prominence through various means—food blogs, cooking shows, cookbooks, and social media—to expose you to a wide range of cuisines and culinary perspectives and, most importantly, help them become more confident (and creative!) cooks.

> **"It is the simplest way to have the greatest chefs in your kitchen."**
> **—Al Roker**

This book contains recipes from those who have made appearances dozens (if not hundreds) of times, known for their tried-and-true techniques, as well as those who have only recently joined us, a new generation of home cooks, offering fresh and exciting methods.

We've evolved as the food world has, but we've never wavered in our goal to deliver accessible, affordable, and comforting recipes that teach you something new—and that's what this book is all about.

Aside from contributions from these culinary leaders, we've included recipes from our own talent—Savannah, Craig, Al, Dylan, Sheinelle, Carson, Jenna, and Hoda—who all have been inspired by the show's cooking segments and prepare meals for their families at home, but they all bring something different to the table.

> **"Doing the cooking segments is one of my favorite memories from my time on the show."**
> **—Hoda Kotb**

Savannah prefers snacking over having a full sit-down meal. Craig is all about comforting, Southern staples inherited from his mom. Al is passionate about high-quality meats and spices. Carson prioritizes big, family-friendly meals. Sheinelle has a solid repertoire of potluck dishes up her sleeve. Dylan is always cooking weeknight meals with her sons. Jenna leans heavily into the Tex-Mex food of her childhood.

> ## "If you're stuck in a meal-making rut, this book will be your best friend!"
> ### —Carson Daly

So, they're kind of all over the place, but nothing brings the talent together more than a cooking segment. As the smell of the food wafts through the studio at 6:30 in the morning, before the show starts, a collective excitement builds among the anchors. Craig and Carson, specifically, are constantly popping into the kitchen during commercial breaks to see what's cooking and hopefully snag a sample.

When we have a chef on the show, they are a big part of the planning process, but they are not actually making the dishes you see so beautifully composed at the end of the segment.

The food stylists make TV magic.

The segment itself will last only four to five minutes—at most—but it takes the food team days, sometimes weeks, of planning and hours of preparation to turn a recipe into a TV-friendly demo with actionable advice.

Our Thanksgiving show, in particular, is the production to end all productions. It's our food team's time to shine. With dozens of all-star chefs and their recipes, it takes months to put together multiple segments across the hours that (we hope) leave our viewers feeling empowered to tackle their holiday cooking. So, of course, we had to include some Thanksgiving-worthy recipes, too (see Erin French's Smoky Tea-Brined Turkey on page 194 and Molly Yeh's Crispy Brussels Sprout Casserole on page 117).

And as soon as a cooking segment is over, you've never seen people move faster than our crew toward the food, with their Tupperware in tow. It's really a marvel to behold. There's nothing like watching hordes of people in the control room and scene dock, who have been seeing and smelling this food for hours, finally get the chance to descend upon the table and taste it.

So, if you've ever wondered what happens to leftover food after a segment, it typically gets snapped up by hungry staffers. In terms of leftover ingredients, though, our lead food stylist Katie Stilo will often whip up some treats in the prep kitchen—like her Scene Dock Schnitzel (page 193) and Apple Cider Doughnut Pancakes (page 31)—for the talent and staff to enjoy behind the scenes.

When we were deciding which recipes to feature in this book, we thought about the dishes that would inspire that type of mad dash.

We don't ask world-renowned chefs who come on the show for their restaurant recipes; we ask them for the recipes they make when they're exhausted on a Sunday after a long week of professional cooking. What do they turn to for comfort? What do they serve their families to show them love? What do they pull out of their back pocket when friends stop by?

> ## "It's the way we get to interact with chefs we admire. It's a window into their world."
> ### —Jenna Bush Hager

Everything in this book is, first and foremost, approachable. The recipes range from no-effort weeknight wonders to special occasion showstoppers, but none contain an overwhelmingly lengthy list of ingredients or steps—we promise. More often than not, you will already have the ingredients and equipment you need for a recipe on hand. But we will show you exciting ways to cook with ingredients you already know and love, and introduce you to some new flavors from around the world, too. Think classic recipes, but with surprising and delightful twists.

A good chunk of this book is reserved for weeknight cooking—because that's what our segments predominantly highlight—to inspire even our busiest viewers to say, "I could actually make that tonight." Think soups, salads, pastas, chicken (lots of chicken!), fish, and entrée-worthy vegetables. And since grilling is our favorite Plaza pastime, expect a good amount of grilled meats. Entertaining and holidays are also essential parts of our show, so we've also got plenty of crowd-pleasing dishes, both sweet and savory. Think dips, savory pies, slow-cooked meats, turkey, starchy sides, and cakes (lots of cakes!).

We hope this book offers you a peek at the way we cook and eat—on-screen, backstage, and at home—and lets you in on some helpful tricks of the trade.

This is a no-judgment zone. No matter where you are on your cooking journey, we are here to help.

But we do want you to step outside of your comfort zone—at least a little.

We hope you keep this book close for when you're feeling uninspired and about to reach for the take-out menu—so you reach for this instead. We hope turning to this book at the end of a long workday becomes as second nature to you as turning on our show when you wake up.

> ## "I've learned so much. When I'm sampling the food, I'm thinking about how I can re-create it at home so my family can enjoy it, too."
> ### —Dylan Dreyer

We realize what a privilege it is to have access to some of the best chefs and home cooks in the world, and we are so excited to bring you recipes that show off each of their culinary specialties, complete with technique tips and suggested swaps. We hope it empowers you to try something new and become a more assertive cook, willing to experiment and diverge from the recipe.

Above all else, though, we hope this book encourages you to spend more time gathered around the table with your loved ones, sharing a meal together—just like we do every morning.

> ## "When you sit at the TODAY table, you're officially part of the best family in television."
> ### —Sheinelle Jones

PRE-PRODUCTION

BEFORE ANY FOOD SEGMENTS CAN HAPPEN, there is so much preparation that needs to be done behind the scenes: pitching, phone calls, recipe editing, writing demo steps, shopping, cooking, set dressing, prop styling, food styling, and more. So, before you dive into this book, we want you to be as prepared as our team is when it's airtime—and that means taking stock of your kitchen.

EQUIPMENT

Our studio kitchen and prop room have more cooking equipment than anyone could even dream of using, because, well, you never know what we're going to need to whip up at a moment's notice. But, knowing that most people don't have that kind of space, we pulled together a list of essentials-only tools we think every home cook should have at the ready.

Knives: Chef's knife (for slicing and chopping meat, vegetables, herbs, and nuts), serrated knife (for slicing bread, cake, pastry, and tough-skinned fruits and vegetables), paring knife (for peeling, coring, and removing stems from fruits and vegetables), and kitchen shears (for breaking down poultry, snipping herbs, and opening food packaging). Keep in mind that a sharp knife is a safe knife (dull knives lead to accidents!), so be sure to get them sharpened regularly.

Seasoning containers: Salt cellar (for quick and easy access to kosher salt, the most commonly used type in cooking and this book) and a pepper mill (because freshly ground pepper has a more robust flavor compared to preground pepper).

Cutting board: A large wood cutting board is your kitchen workhorse—it's durable, gentle on knives, and has natural antimicrobial properties.

Strainers: Fine-mesh sieve (for draining canned beans and vegetables, straining liquids, and sifting dry ingredients) and colander (for draining pasta, grains, and legumes and rinsing produce).

Graters and peelers: Box grater (for grating cheese and shredding vegetables), Microplane (for grating garlic, ginger, cheese, whole spices, and chocolate, and zesting citrus) and Y-peeler (for peeling fruits and vegetables, shaving chocolate and cheese, and making citrus strips to garnish cocktails).

Other utensils: Fish spatula (for flipping fish, eggs, burgers, pancakes, really anything), offset spatula (for frosting cakes and spreading fillings), silicone spatula (for mixing and folding ingredients, scraping bowls and cookware, and spreading batter), pastry brush (for applying sauces, oils, glazes, and other liquids), balloon whisk (for whipping, beating, and aerating ingredients like eggs, cream, or batters), flat whisk (for deglazing pans and stirring sauces), metal tongs (for lifting, flipping, tossing, and serving foods), and slotted spoon (for retrieving solids from a cooking liquid).

Measuring tools: Dry measuring cups, liquid measuring cup, measuring spoons, kitchen scale (especially if you're an avid baker), digital meat thermometer, and candy thermometer (not just for candy-making but for deep-frying, too).

Pots and pans: Small (6 to 8 inches/15 to 20 cm) and large (10 to 12 inches/25 to 30.5 cm) skillets (stainless steel or nonstick is up to you!), 3- to 3½-quart (3 to 3.5 L) straight-sided sauté pan (for shallow-frying and low-liquid braising), 10- to 12-inch (25 to 30.5 cm) cast-iron skillet (for searing, frying, and baking), large Dutch oven (for braising meat and vegetables, cooking soups and stews, and baking bread), 2- to 4-quart (2 to 4 L) saucepan (for heating soups and sauces, boiling water, and cooking grains).

Sheet pans: Half-sheet pan (18 by 13-inch/46 by 33 cm) and quarter-sheet pan (13 by 9-inch/ 33 by 23 cm)—for baking and roasting anything and everything. They can also be used as serving, meal-prep, thawing, and breading trays.

Casserole dish: We love a casserole here at *TODAY*, so of course we're going to recommend this. You can't go wrong with glass or ceramic, but we prefer ceramic for its ability to retain heat more evenly.

Food processor or high-powered blender: If you plan on making any thick and creamy dips, spreads, soups, or sauces, you should probably have one.

SUPPLIES

The right cooking tools are crucial, but they will get you nowhere without ingredients. Keeping all the recipes in this book in mind, we compiled this list of foods to stock your pantry, fridge, and freezer with. It's by no means an exhaustive guide but rather a starter pack. You'll still have to pop out to the store to grab some things, but you'll have a solid foundation at home.

Oils: Extra-virgin olive, neutral (vegetable, canola, or grapeseed)

Vinegars: Red wine, rice, balsamic, apple cider

Seasonings: Kosher salt (we use Diamond Crystal), black peppercorns, red pepper flakes (see page 197 for Al's spice guide)

Frozen: Chicken (thighs, breasts, and wings), fish fillets (such as salmon and cod), sausages, ground beef and pork, bacon, spinach, peas

Produce: Garlic, onions, shallots, lemons, limes, potatoes (Yukon Gold or russet), carrots, celery, tofu, parsley, cilantro, scallions, ginger

Dairy: Eggs, unsalted butter, milk, heavy cream, buttermilk, yogurt, sour cream, cheeses (Parmesan or pecorino, cheddar, Swiss or Gruyère, feta)

Canned and jarred: Whole peeled tomatoes, coconut milk, anchovies, tuna, pickles, capers, olives, kimchi, chickpeas, cannellini beans, black beans, boxed chicken/beef/vegetable stock

Condiments and sauces: Ketchup, mustard (yellow and Dijon), mayonnaise, hot sauces, miso, soy sauce, Worcestershire sauce, fish sauce, ponzu, peanut butter, tahini, salsa, harissa, chili oil/crisp

Nuts: Cashews, walnuts, pistachios, peanuts, almonds

Sweeteners: Honey, maple syrup, granulated sugar

Grains and starches: Rice (short- and long-grain), pasta (short and long), ramen, seasoned dried bread crumbs, panko bread crumbs

Baking: All-purpose flour, cake flour, rolled oats, powdered sugar, brown sugar (light and dark), baking soda, baking powder, cornstarch, vanilla extract, bittersweet baking chocolate, semisweet chocolate chips

"I don't say this lightly, but the food segments are probably my favorite part of the show."

—Craig Melvin

Morning Boost:
BREAKFAST

Just like watching the show, breakfast can set the tone for your day—and all of these recipes will get you off on the right foot. Whether you wake up craving something sweet (pancakes, anyone?) or savory (cheesy strata, perhaps?), we've got something to satisfy you. You'll find a couple of elixirs, too: For a nasty hangover, turn to Carson's famous Bloody Mary (page 38); for a warm hug in a mug, curl up with Sheinelle's ginger-honey-lemon tea (page 21). Regardless of the forecast, these dishes will bring the sunshine.

Ina Garten's
PERFECT GRUYÈRE & HERB OMELET

SERVES 1
PREP TIME: 5 MINUTES
COOK TIME: 5 MINUTES

3 extra-large eggs

½ teaspoon kosher salt, plus more for serving

¼ teaspoon freshly ground black pepper, plus more for serving

1 tablespoon minced fresh herbs, such as dill, parsley, and chives, plus more for serving

1 tablespoon unsalted butter

1 tablespoon canola oil

¼ cup (25 g) grated aged Gruyère cheese

Ina has spent her life in pursuit of the perfect omelet. She's tried every method in the book, but they'd turn out either too browned, too dense, or too hard to roll. But after seeing French chef Jacques Pépin make one, she had an egg-piphany. Everything fell into place, and she was left with something delicate yet decadent at the same time. The key is high-quality ingredients (if you can't churn your own butter, store-bought is fine*) and, of course, technique (keep the eggs constantly in motion!). Ina ups the creaminess ante by adding Gruyere cheese, then cooks the omelet until just set on the outside. How fabulous is that?

*This is a *Barefoot Contessa*—based joke, in case that wasn't clear.

In a bowl, vigorously whisk the eggs, 1 tablespoon water, the salt, and pepper until smooth. Add the herbs and beat to combine.

In a 9-inch (23 cm) nonstick skillet, warm the butter and oil over medium heat. Just before the butter completely melts, pour in the egg mixture and immediately, while shaking the pan, rapidly stir the eggs with the back of a fork (as if you were making scrambled eggs) until the eggs are almost, but not totally cooked, 30 to 60 seconds.

Using the back of the fork, spread the mixture into an even layer, allowing the eggs to form a thin layer on the bottom of the pan, about 10 seconds.

Meanwhile, sprinkle the cheese down the middle of the omelet.

With a heatproof spatula, fold the sides of the omelet over the cheese as if you were folding a letter, first one side and then the other, so they overlap.

Invert the omelet onto a plate, garnish with herbs, and finish with a light sprinkling of salt and pepper. Serve hot.

 TIP

If you're making a few omelets, have all the egg mixtures and other ingredients prepped before you start cooking the first one.

Sheinelle's
GINGER HONEY LEMON ELIXIR

SERVES 6
PREP TIME: 10 MINUTES
COOK TIME: 20 MINUTES
INACTIVE TIME: 12 HOURS

2 large lemons, halved

1 cup (125 g) sliced fresh ginger (¼-inch/6 mm) coins

½ cup (120 ml) raw honey

Lemon wedges, for serving

Over the years, Sheinelle has had all sorts of throat issues, even undergoing throat surgery years ago. So, if something doesn't feel right, especially right before she has to go on the air, she has to quickly remedy the situation. For years, she would run into the green room, grab a cup of hot water, stir in honey, and drink it. One day, Katie, our head food stylist, inquired about this ritual and offered to whip her up something proper—this ginger-honey-lemon tea—and the rest is history. Now, Sheinelle will just give Katie a look and she'll know to bring it to her. "I'll be honest, some days, it has nothing to do with my vocal health," says Sheinelle. "It's just comforting and warm and helps me relax before the show."

Fill a 3-quart (3 L) saucepan with 6 cups (1.4 L) cold water. Squeeze the juice from the lemons directly into the saucepan, then add the halves to the pot along with the ginger. Bring to a simmer over medium heat and cook for 15 minutes.

Transfer to a heatproof container, cool to room temperature, then refrigerate overnight.

Strain the mixture into a saucepan, add the honey, and warm, stirring to dissolve the honey, to your desired temperature.

Ladle into teacups and serve with a wedge of lemon.

Tina DeGraff Martinez's
SWEET & SALTY GRANOLA

MAKES ABOUT 8 CUPS
PREP TIME: 10 MINUTES
COOK TIME: 35 MINUTES
INACTIVE TIME: 1 HOUR (COOLING)

2½ cups (220 g) rolled oats

⅓ cup (40 g) all-purpose flour

½ cup (60 g) chopped pecans

½ cup (50 g) sliced almonds

½ cup (65 g) chopped cashews

½ cup (30 g) unsweetened coconut flakes

1½ teaspoons kosher salt

1½ teaspoons ground cinnamon

¼ cup (60 ml) coconut oil, melted

½ cup (120 ml) maple syrup

5 large Medjool dates, pitted and roughly chopped

There was nothing better than walking into Studio 1A at 5:00 a.m. and being embraced by the warm scent of our former food stylist Tina's granola baking in the oven. She used to make it for every chef who came on the show, and we're convinced that's why so many kept coming back. "When Tina made it, she knew to triple the quantity because we would all fight over who got to take some home," says Katie, our lead food stylist. Unlike most overly sweet and sticky store-bought granola, Tina's is the perfect balance of sweet and salty, crunchy and chewy.

Preheat the oven to 350°F (180°C). Line a half-sheet pan with parchment paper.

In a large bowl, toss together the oats, flour, pecans, almonds, cashers, coconut, salt, and cinnamon. Add the coconut oil and maple syrup and toss well, ensuring all the dry ingredients are fully coated with the wet ingredients. Spread the mixture onto the prepared sheet pan.

Bake for 15 minutes. With a large spatula, toss the granola, then bake for 10 minutes more. Add the dates, toss once more to combine, and bake until deep golden brown, about 8 minutes.

Cool for 1 hour before breaking into clusters.

Store in an airtight container at room temperature for up to 2 weeks or in the freezer for up to 3 months.

 TIP

Use kitchen shears to cut the dates into pieces without sticking!

Elizabeth Poett's
FRENCH ONION STRATA

SERVES 8
PREP TIME: 20 MINUTES
COOK TIME: 1 HOUR 30 MINUTES
INACTIVE TIME: 6 HOURS
**   45 MINUTES**

Softened butter, for the casserole dish

1 large loaf French bread, cut into ½-inch (12 mm) slices

4 tablespoons (55 g) unsalted butter

2 tablespoons extra-virgin olive oil

4 medium sweet onions, thinly sliced (about 4 cups/960 ml)

4 teaspoons kosher salt

2 tablespoons sugar

2 tablespoons white wine (optional)

1 teaspoon chopped fresh thyme, plus more for garnish

12 large eggs

3 cups (720 ml) half-and-half

¼ teaspoon freshly ground black pepper

14 ounces (400 g) Gruyère cheese, shredded

French onion soup meets savory bread pudding in this absolute showstopper of a breakfast. It's everything you love about the soup, with its sweet caramelized onions, browned, bubbling cheese, and crusty French bread, but in the form of a crowd-pleasing casserole. The best part about it, according to Elizabeth, author of *The Ranch Table* cookbook, is that you can prep it the night before and pop it in the oven in the morning for a stress-free (yet incredibly impressive-looking) brunch for guests.

Preheat the oven to 350°F (180°C). Grease a 9 by 13-inch (22 by 33 cm) casserole dish with some softened butter.

Lay the bread slices on a sheet pan and bake until golden brown and mostly dried out, about 20 minutes. Set aside.

Meanwhile, in a large deep skillet, melt the butter in the olive oil over medium heat. Add the onions and cook until soft and tender, about 10 minutes.

Add 2 teaspoons of the salt, the sugar, and white wine (if using) and cook, stirring occasionally, until the onions are deep brown, about 35 minutes.

Add the thyme, stir to combine, and cook for 1 minute. Remove from the heat.

Meanwhile, in a large bowl, whisk the eggs until smooth. Add the half-and-half, the remaining 2 teaspoons salt, and the pepper and whisk to combine.

Line the prepared casserole dish with half of the toasted bread. Scatter half of the onion mixture evenly over the bread. Sprinkle half of the Gruyère evenly over the onions. Repeat the layering with the remaining toast, onion mixture, and cheese.

Recipe continues

Slowly pour the egg mixture evenly over the contents of the casserole dish. Cover with plastic wrap and refrigerate for at least 6 hours, preferably overnight.

Preheat the oven to 350°F (180°C).

Let the casserole sit at room temperature for 30 to 60 minutes. Remove the plastic wrap and cover the dish tightly with foil.

Bake for 1 hour. Remove the foil and bake until the top is golden brown and the strata is bubbling, 20 to 25 minutes.

Let sit for 15 minutes before serving with a garnish of fresh thyme.

Katie Stilo's
APPLE CIDER DOUGHNUT PANCAKES

SERVES 4
PREP TIME: 10 MINUTES
COOK TIME: 35 MINUTES

FOR THE TOPPING

¼ cup (50 g) sugar

2 teaspoons ground cinnamon

FOR THE PANCAKES

2 cups (240 g) all-purpose flour

3 tablespoons sugar

2 teaspoons baking powder

½ teaspoon baking soda

1 teaspoon ground cinnamon

1 teaspoon kosher salt

2 large eggs

1 cup (240 ml) buttermilk

¾ cup (180 ml) apple cider

1 teaspoon vanilla extract

Unsalted butter, for cooking the pancakes

FOR SERVING (OPTIONAL)

Apple butter

Chopped pecans or walnuts

Whipped cream

MAKE AHEAD

You can cook the pancakes and freeze them in individual zip-top bags—just reheat in the oven or toaster whenever the craving strikes.

Every year, when fall rolls around, the studio seems to be overflowing with apple cider. We use it in various segments for cocktails, sauces, desserts, and more. One day, after a week of these segments, our lead food stylist Katie had to think of a way to use up the leftover cider we had, and since it was six in the morning, her mind was on pancakes. She tweaked her classic pancake recipe to include cider instead of milk, and it only took the flip of one flapjack for the talent to come wandering in during a commercial break to see what was cooking. These were an instant hit. With a caramelized cinnamon sugar topping, they evoke the warm doughnuts from the farmstand on a crisp fall day.

Make the topping: In a small bowl, mix the sugar and cinnamon to combine. Set aside.

Make the pancakes: Preheat a nonstick small (6 to 8 inches/15 to 20 cm) skillet over medium-low heat.

Meanwhile, in a medium bowl, whisk together the flour, sugar, baking powder, baking soda, cinnamon, and salt.

In another medium bowl, beat the eggs until smooth. Whisk in the buttermilk, apple cider, and vanilla.

Add the wet ingredients to the dry and whisk, mixing just until there are no streaks of dry ingredients remaining (small lumps are good!).

Recipe continues

Add 1 tablespoon of butter to the skillet and swirl to coat the bottom of the pan. Using a paper towel, gently wipe out any excess butter, leaving just a very light layer of fat in the skillet.

Scoop ⅓ cup (75 ml) of the batter into the center of the skillet. Sprinkle ½ teaspoon of the topping evenly over the pancake and cook until bubbles appear all over the surface, about 3 minutes. Flip and cook until set, about 1 minute. Transfer to a plate and keep warm.

Repeat with the remaining batter, wiping the skillet clean with paper towels in between each pancake, and greasing as needed.

To serve, drizzle some melted butter on top with apple butter, chopped nuts, and whipped cream, if desired. Sprinkle with cinnamon sugar to finish, if you like.

SAVORY FRENCH TOAST LASAGNA

Ali Rosen's

SERVES 4
PREP TIME: 10 MINUTES
COOK TIME: 30 MINUTES

3 large eggs

½ cup (120 ml) heavy cream

½ teaspoon kosher salt

1 loaf challah, cut into 1-inch-thick (2.5 cm) slices

1 (7-ounce/198 g) package breakfast sausage links, sliced

½ cup (50 g) finely grated Parmesan cheese

Handful of chopped or ripped basil leaves

Maple syrup

French toast, but make it savory. Lasagna, but make it breakfast. This recipe breaks a lot of rules, but rules are meant to be broken. Why shouldn't you soak bread in eggs and heavy cream and then layer it, lasagna-style, with sausage and cheese? Why shouldn't you make it in advance and pop it in the oven for a crowd-pleasing breakfast or dinner? Ali, author of *15 Minute Meals*, is here to tell you that you absolutely should—and you'll be happy you didn't stick to the rules.

Preheat the oven to 350°F (180°C). Grease a 9 by 13-inch (22 by 33 cm) baking dish with cooking spray.

In a shallow bowl, beat the eggs until smooth. Add the cream and salt and whisk to combine.

Begin dipping the bread into the egg mixture, making sure each slice is fully soaked, placing the slices into a single layer in the prepared baking dish.

Once the bottom of the dish is fully covered, sprinkle the sausage slices, half of the Parmesan, and some basil evenly over the bread. Layer the remaining soaked bread over the sausage. Sprinkle the remaining cheese evenly over the top.

Bake until golden brown and the bread is no longer wet, 25 to 30 minutes.

Serve hot with a sprinkling of basil and a drizzle of maple syrup.

Carson's
MAGICAL HANGOVER-CURING BLOODY MARY

MAKES 1 COCKTAIL
PREP TIME: 5 MINUTES

Ice

½ cup (120 ml) Bloody Mary mix, such as Mr & Mrs T Original

3 ounces (90 ml) Ketel One vodka

2 teaspoons Worcestershire sauce

1½ teaspoons prepared horseradish

1 teaspoon bread-and-butter pickle juice, such as Bubbies

1 teaspoon fresh lemon juice

3 dashes of hot sauce

Pinch of celery salt

Pinch of freshly ground black pepper

Beef jerky, for garnish

Celery stalk, for garnish

Lemon wedge, for garnish

"It will surprise nobody that I have had a few hangovers in my day," says Carson. So, over the years, he's developed the ultimate antidote to a night of overindulgence—this magical concoction. The secret ingredient is pickle juice, which contains electrolytes that can help rehydrate your body. And a splash of beef broth takes it from a Bloody Mary closer to a Bloody Bull, a drink rumored to have originated at Brennan's in New Orleans. Garnished with beef jerky and celery, it's **"a drink that will make you feel better immediately,"** he says. **"Within 10 seconds—guaranteed."**

Fill a pint glass with a lot of ice. Add the Bloody Mary mix, vodka, Worcestershire, horseradish, pickle juice, lemon juice, and hot sauce and stir to combine. Add more ice to fill the glass, as needed.

Sprinkle the celery salt and pepper over the top. Garnish with beef jerky, a celery stalk, and a lemon wedge.

 TIP

Use lots of ice and mix until very cold.

Sound Bites:
SNACKS & APPS

We'll be right back after this snack break. Between segments, we're always snacking on something in the scene dock. Savannah, especially, lives on finger food, so she'll show you how to make her cheese plate, pigs in a blanket, and guacamole, which she commonly serves with Jenna's queso while sipping on a Savanita. You'll find plenty of ideas for entertaining—especially tailgating— from Carson's pizza to Siri's pull-apart sliders. Consider your guests' appetites whetted.

Savannah's
GO-TO GUAC

MAKES ABOUT 3 CUPS; SERVES 6
PREP TIME: 10 MINUTES

4 medium Hass avocados (about 1¾ pounds/795 g total), diced

¼ cup (35 g) finely diced red onion

¼ cup (45 g) finely diced seeded Roma tomatoes (optional)

¼ cup (10 g) finely chopped fresh cilantro

¼ cup (60 ml) fresh lime juice

1 teaspoon kosher salt, plus more to taste

¼ teaspoon freshly ground black pepper

Tortilla chips, for serving

To Savannah, guac is not just a snack or a side—it's the main event. "I eat it for breakfast, lunch, and dinner," she says. "I pair it with a Savanita (recipe follows) and I'm good to go on a weeknight." Her take on Texas ranch water, the Savanita combines tequila, lots of lime juice (always fresh, never bottled), sparkling water, and ice. As for the guac, it's nothing fancy—and that's the beauty of it. All you need is avocado, onion, cilantro, and lime juice to make a dip that'll have you reaching for the tortilla chip remnants at the bottom of the bag.

In a large bowl, mash the avocado until chunky. Add the red onion, tomatoes (if using), cilantro, lime juice, salt, and pepper and stir to combine. Taste and season with more salt if needed.

Transfer to a serving bowl and serve with tortilla chips.

SAVANITA

MAKES 1 COCKTAIL
PREP TIME: 5 MINUTES

Ice

2 ounces (60 ml) tequila blanco

1½ ounces (45 ml) fresh lime juice

Club soda

Lime wedge

Load a rocks glass with ice cubes. Add the tequila and lime juice and stir with a cocktail spoon to combine. Top with the club soda. Garnish with a lime wedge and serve immediately.

 TIP

Want to turn up the heat? Add ¼ cup diced jalapeños to the guac.

Jenna's
QUESO TO END ALL QUESOS

MAKES ABOUT 8 CUPS; SERVES 16
PREP TIME: 10 MINUTES
COOK TIME: 15 MINUTES

2 tablespoons canola oil

1 small yellow onion (about 6 ounces/170 g), finely diced

1 pound (455 g) ground beef (80/20)

1 (1-ounce/28 g) packet mild taco seasoning

1 (16-ounce/455 g) block processed cheese, such as Velveeta, cut into cubes

1 (10-ounce/285 g) can diced tomatoes & green chilies, such as Ro-tel

1 (16-ounce/455 g) can refried beans

2 avocados (6 ounces/170 g each), diced

Chips, for serving

Jenna ate *a lot* of queso growing up. "It's basically considered a food group in Texas," she says. When her mom wasn't making Tex-Mex at home, they'd go out to eat Tex-Mex. Her signature queso recipe is a remix of the Bob Armstrong dip at Magnolia Cafe in Austin. It has everything—beef, cheese, tomatoes, green chiles, beans, and avocado—and couldn't be easier to make. Just dump it all into a pot and within 10 minutes you'll achieve ooey-gooey gloriousness. "This is the dip of all dips," says Jenna. "Make it and everybody will be very happy."

In a heavy-bottomed 3-quart (3 L) pot, heat the oil over medium-high heat. Add the onion and sauté, stirring constantly, until softened, 2 to 3 minutes.

Add the ground beef and cook, breaking the meat into small pieces with a wooden spoon, until browned, about 4 minutes. Sprinkle the taco seasoning over the meat, stir to combine, and cook, stirring constantly, for 1 minute.

Reduce the heat to medium and add the Velveeta, Ro-tel, and refried beans and cook, stirring occasionally, until the cheese is completely melted and all the ingredients are warmed through, about 5 minutes.

Remove from the heat, add the avocado, and stir to combine.

Gently pour the queso into a serving bowl and serve with your favorite chips—or enjoy by the spoonful!

 TIP

Want to spice it up? Top it with jalapeño slices, like Jenna's husband, Henry, does.

Siri Daly's
PULL-APART
MONTE CRISTO SLIDERS

SERVES 12
PREP TIME: 15 MINUTES
COOK TIME: 30 MINUTES

4 tablespoons (55 g) unsalted butter, melted

1 teaspoon mustard powder

1½ teaspoons Worcestershire sauce

1 (12-ounce/240 g) package Hawaiian sweet rolls (do not pull them apart)

½ cup (120 ml) mayonnaise

2 teaspoons Dijon mustard

½ pound (225 g) deli-sliced ham

½ pound (225 g) deli-sliced turkey

½ pound (225 g) sliced Swiss cheese

Powdered sugar

Siri's mom's friend Lucy used to light up rooms with her smile and sticky ham sandwiches. She passed away far too young from Alzheimer's but lives on in so many ways—including as the inspiration for this recipe. Siri's sliders are a hybrid of Lucy's famous dish and the Monte Cristo, making for a pull-apart, crowd-pleasing take on the battered and fried turkey, ham, and cheese sandwich. Set down a tray of these sweet and savory bites at your tailgate and it'll be empty in a matter of moments—guaranteed. (Just don't forget the napkins!)

Preheat the oven to 325°F (160°C).

In a small bowl, whisk together the melted butter, mustard powder, and Worcestershire sauce. Brush a 7 by 11-inch (17 by 28 cm) baking dish with some of the butter mixture.

Using a serrated knife, slice the buns horizontally in half (see Tip). Separate the tops from the bottoms and place the bottom half into the prepared baking dish.

In a small bowl, mix the mayonnaise and Dijon mustard to combine and spread half evenly over the bottom layer of the rolls. Layer the ham and turkey evenly over the rolls. Layer the cheese over the meat. Spread the remaining mayonnaise mixture onto the underside of the top half of the buns and place it over the cheese.

Brush the butter mixture over the rolls and drizzle any remaining mixture evenly over the top. Loosely cover with foil.

Bake for 20 minutes. Remove the foil and bake until the tops are lightly toasted and the cheese is melted, 10 to 15 minutes.

Use a serrated knife to cut into individual sandwiches. Sprinkle with a generous coating of powdered sugar and serve.

 TIP

Sweet Hawaiian buns are easy to slice all at once as long as you use a long serrated knife and don't pull them apart before cutting.

Carson's
LOADED BAKED POTATO PIZZAS

MAKES 2 SMALL PIZZAS; SERVES 4
PREP TIME: 15 MINUTES
COOK TIME: 10 MINUTES
INACTIVE TIME: 30 MINUTES

2 small Yukon Gold potatoes
(6 ounces/170 g total)

1-pound (455 g) ball pizza dough

¼ cup (60 ml) sour cream

All-purpose flour, for dusting

8 ounces (225 g) mild cheddar
cheese, grated on the large holes
of a box grater

1 cup (50 g) crumbled crispy
cooked bacon

Fresh chives, finely chopped

Flaky sea salt and freshly ground
black pepper

Pizza night is a family affair in the Daly household. Carson's wife, Siri, makes the dough the night before. The next day they'll set up stations with toppings, their son, Jackson, will roll out the dough and the Daly girls will scatter (and snack on) the mozzarella cheese. After countless pizza nights, Carson says, "We've gotten very experimental," and that's how this over-the-top pie came to be. Imagine everything in a loaded baked potato—crumbled bacon, shredded cheddar, chopped chives, and a sour cream drizzle—in pizza form. "We never really thought it would be as good as it has turned out to be," he says. "But it's really, really good."

Place a pizza stone on the lower rack of the oven and preheat the oven to 500°F (260°C).

Using a mandoline, thinly slice the potatoes into a large bowl filled with cold water.

In a small bowl, stir the sour cream with 2 teaspoons cold water to create a sauce.

Divide the pizza dough into 2 equal portions and shape each into a ball. Using your fingers, on a lightly floured surface, stretch each one into a rough round. Cover with a clean kitchen towel and let rest for 10 minutes.

Continue shaping each dough into a rough round about 10 inches (25 cm) across. Cover with the kitchen towel and let sit for another 10 minutes.

Working with one round of dough at a time, give it a final stretch, shaping it into a 12-inch (30 cm) round (see Tip). Let sit, covered, for 5 minutes.

Transfer one pizza crust to a lightly floured pizza peel. Sprinkle half of the cheddar over the pizza, leaving a 1-inch (2.5 cm) border all around. Using paper towels, pat half of the potatoes to dry and stagger them over the cheese.

Recipe continues

 TIP

If the pizza dough is difficult to
work with and is retracting when
stretched, cover the dough and
let it rest in 10-minute increments.

Slide the pizza onto the pizza stone and bake until the cheese is bubbling and the crust is golden brown, spinning it front to back halfway through, 8 to 10 minutes.

Transfer to a wire rack. Sprinkle with half the bacon and drizzle with half of the sour cream sauce. Add a sprinkling of chives, salt, and pepper. Serve hot.

Repeat to make the second pizza.

Hetty Lui McKinnon's
Hetty Lui McKinnon's
MISO MUSHROOM GALETTE

SERVES 4
PREP TIME: 35 MINUTES
COOK TIME: 30 MINUTES
INACTIVE TIME: 40 MINUTES

FOR THE BLACK PEPPER DOUGH

1¾ cups (225 g) all-purpose flour, plus more for dusting

1 teaspoon sea salt

½ teaspoon freshly ground black pepper

1 stick (4 ounces/115 g) cold unsalted butter, cut into ⅓ inch (1 cm) pieces

⅓ to ½ cup (80 to 120 ml) ice-cold water

FOR THE MISO MUSHROOM FILLING

1 pound (455 g) mixed mushrooms, such as cremini, shiitake, trumpet, and oyster

Extra-virgin olive oil

2 tablespoons white (shiro) miso

2 tablespoons unsalted butter

1 clove garlic, grated

FOR ASSEMBLY

3 scallions, thinly sliced

1 cup (245 g) whole-milk ricotta cheese

Sea salt and freshly ground black pepper

1 large egg, beaten

Handful of toasted sesame seeds (black, white or both)

This bold, savory galette will attract a crowd, no matter the occasion—it's simple enough to prepare as a weeknight dinner but special enough to serve on a holiday table. While everyday cremini mushrooms work well here, *Tenderheart* cookbook author Hetty likes to experiment with different types of mushrooms—in particular, shiitakes and royal trumpets—to add a greater depth of flavor and variety of textures. Miso brings the magic: The fermented, sweet and savory notes of the paste bolster the umami in the mushrooms. Delicate, flaky, and simple to put together, the black pepper dough is good to have up your sleeve for future savory galettes this one will inevitably inspire you to make.

Make the black pepper dough: In a medium bowl, whisk together the flour, salt, and pepper. Add the butter and toss to combine. Using your fingertips, squeeze the butter to flatten the pieces. Do not worry if the butter pieces are not uniform in size.

Add ¼ cup (60 ml) of the water and, using your hands, toss to hydrate the flour. Continue adding some water, a little bit at a time, mixing just until the dough comes together; it should not be sticky. Shape the dough into a flat disc, wrap in plastic wrap, and refrigerate until chilled, about 30 minutes, or up to overnight.

Meanwhile, make the miso mushroom filling: Prepare the mushrooms by thickly slicing any large ones and leave the smaller ones whole.

In a large skillet, heat 2 tablespoons olive oil over medium-high heat. Add the mushrooms and cook, stirring every few minutes, until lightly golden brown, 6 to 7 minutes.

Reduce the heat to low, add the miso, butter, and garlic, and cook, tossing as needed, until the mushrooms are evenly coated, about 2 minutes. Remove from the heat and transfer to a plate to cool for 5 to 10 minutes.

Recipe continues

Preheat the oven to 400°F (200°C).

To assemble: Set aside a small handful of scallions for garnish. In a small bowl, stir the ricotta with the remaining scallions, until combined. Season with salt and pepper to taste.

Place the dough onto the center of a sheet of parchment paper and sprinkle the top with a light dusting of flour. Roll the dough into a rough round about 12 inches (30 cm) in diameter.

Spread the ricotta mixture evenly over the dough, leaving a 1-inch (2.5 cm) border around the edge. Scatter the mushrooms evenly over the ricotta and drizzle with some olive oil.

Using the parchment paper as a guide, gently fold the edges of the dough inward over the filling, pinching together any tears in the dough. Brush the egg over the exposed crust and scatter the sesame seeds over the whole galette.

Bake until the crust is golden brown, 30 to 35 minutes.

Let rest for 10 to 15 minutes before garnishing with the reserved scallions, slicing, and serving.

 TIPS

To ensure an airy crust, make sure you use ice-cold water, always keep the dough cold, and work the dough as little as possible.

If chilling the dough overnight, allow it to sit at room temperature for 20 minutes before rolling.

The galette can be eaten warm or at room temperature.

Kwame Onwuachi's
CREOLE CRAB DIP

SERVES 8
PREP TIME: 10 MINUTES
COOK TIME: 30 MINUTES
INACTIVE TIME: 10 MINUTES

¼ cup (20 g) crushed butter crackers

½ cup (50 g) finely grated Parmigiano-Reggiano cheese

8 ounces (225 g) cream cheese, at room temperature

¾ cup (180 ml) mayonnaise

1 pound (455 g) jumbo lump crabmeat, picked over to remove bits of shell or cartilage

5 scallions, thinly sliced, white and light-green parts kept separate from dark green

1½ teaspoons minced garlic

2 teaspoons Worcestershire sauce

1 tablespoon fresh lemon juice

1 tablespoon Creole seasoning

1 tablespoon Louisiana-style hot sauce, such as Crystal

2 teaspoons Creole mustard

Tortilla chips, for serving

Kwame's family is from Louisiana, which means when they get together, there are snacks and canapes "on every surface of the house," the chef at New York City's Tatiana says—including this dip. One of his mom's signature dishes, it's a creamy, zesty, spicy, buttery delight that is always the first thing to go at a party. You can make the mixture a day in advance and pop it in the oven as guests arrive for a guaranteed "Something smells good in here."

Preheat the oven to 350°F (180°C). Grease a 1½-quart (950 ml) baking dish with cooking spray.

In a small bowl, stir together the crackers and 3 tablespoons (20 g) of the Parmigiano-Reggiano to combine. Set aside.

In a large bowl, stir together the cream cheese and mayonnaise until well combined.

Add the crabmeat, white and light-green scallions, garlic, Worcestershire sauce, lemon juice, Creole seasoning, hot sauce, Creole mustard, and remaining 5 tablespoons (30 g) of the Parmigiano-Reggiano and mix until just combined.

Transfer the mixture to the prepared baking dish and spread it evenly across the dish. Sprinkle the butter cracker mixture evenly over the top.

Bake until golden brown and bubbling, about 30 minutes. Increase the temperature to broil and broil until deep golden brown, 1 to 2 minutes.

Let rest for 10 to 15 minutes before garnishing with the dark-green scallions. Serve with tortilla chips.

Rōze Traore's

HARISSA SHRIMP WITH TOASTED SOURDOUGH

SERVES 2
PREP TIME: 15 MINUTES
COOK TIME: 10 MINUTES

1 tablespoon plus 1 teaspoon extra-virgin olive oil

1 clove garlic, minced

1 tablespoon harissa paste

Grated zest and juice of ½ lemon

2 tablespoons finely chopped fresh basil, plus more for serving

1 teaspoon kosher salt, plus more for sprinkling

½ pound (225 g) jumbo shrimp, peeled, deveined, and patted dry

2 slices sourdough bread, cut on the bias

1 tablespoon unsalted butter

Flaky sea salt, such as Maldon

Lemon wedges, for squeezing

If you're not cooking with harissa, you should be. The spicy North African chile paste is made from a blend of roasted red peppers, hot chile peppers, garlic, olive oil, and aromatic spices and lends fiery flavor to dishes. Here, chef and entrepreneur Rōze uses it alongside garlic, lemon, and butter to make a punchy pan sauce for shrimp. No need to concern yourself with sides, nor utensils, for that matter—just toast up a slice of sourdough to sop up the sauce and you've got yourself dinner.

In a medium sauté pan, heat 1 tablespoon of the olive over medium-high heat. Add the garlic and sauté, stirring constantly, until lightly browned, about 1 minute. Reduce the heat to low, add the harissa paste, lemon zest, lemon juice, basil, kosher salt, and 1 tablespoon water and stir to form a loose sauce.

Add the shrimp and cook until bright pink and cooked through, about 6 minutes, flipping them over halfway through.

Meanwhile, in a large skillet, heat the remaining 1 teaspoon olive oil over medium heat, swirling it to coat the bottom. Add the bread and toast until golden brown on each side, about 2 minutes per side. Spread the butter on the toast.

To serve, divide the toasted bread between two shallow serving bowls and sprinkle with kosher salt. Spoon the shrimp and sauce over the bread and garnish with flaky sea salt and fresh basil. Serve with lemon wedges for squeezing.

Jernard Wells's
HONEY LEMON PEPPER PERI-PERI WINGS

SERVES 6
PREP TIME: 10 MINUTES
COOK TIME: 30 MINUTES

FOR THE WINGS

Vegetable oil, for deep-frying

1 cup (125 g) all-purpose flour

3 tablespoons cornstarch

1 tablespoon lemon-pepper seasoning

1 tablespoon all-purpose seasoning

3 pounds (1.4 kg) chicken wings, cut into drumettes and flats, wing tips removed

FOR THE PERI-PERI SAUCE

5 fresh red chile peppers, stems removed

1 red bell pepper, roughly chopped

4 cloves garlic, peeled

1 teaspoon smoked paprika

1 teaspoon dried oregano

1 teaspoon ground cumin

½ cup (120 ml) extra-virgin olive oil

½ cup (120 ml) honey

Juice of 2 lemons

1 teaspoon kosher salt

1 teaspoon freshly ground black pepper

FOR SERVING

Ranch dressing

"Proceed with caution," says Jernard, chef and host of *New Soul Kitchen*. "These wings are highly addictive." Dredged in a lemon pepper/flour mixture, fried until golden, and tossed in a honey peri-peri sauce, they are a smoky-sweet zest fest. In particular, the peri-peri sauce, a Portuguese-African condiment popular in Angola, Mozambique, and South Africa, will require major finger-licking. You have been warned.

Cook the wings: Line a baking sheet with paper towels and set near the stove. Fill a deep-fryer or large Dutch oven, halfway up, with vegetable oil and preheat to 375°F (190°C).

In a large bowl, whisk together the flour, cornstarch, lemon-pepper seasoning, and all-purpose seasoning until well combined.

Dredge the chicken wing parts in the flour mixture, making sure they are evenly and fully coated, shaking off any excess flour.

Working in batches, fry the chicken wings, in batches, until golden brown and cooked through, 10 to 12 minutes. Transfer to the paper towels to drain.

Meanwhile, make the peri-peri sauce: In a blender or food processor, process the chiles, bell pepper, garlic, smoked paprika, oregano, cumin, olive oil, honey, lemon juice, salt, and black pepper, scraping down the sides as needed, until smooth.

In a large bowl, toss the wings in the peri-peri sauce until evenly coated. Serve hot with ranch dressing.

Savannah's
GARLIC BREAD
PIGS IN A BLANKET

SERVES 6
PREP TIME: 15 MINUTES
COOK TIME: 10 MINUTES

FOR THE GARLIC BUTTER

6 tablespoons (85 g) unsalted butter, at room temperature

4 cloves garlic, grated on a Microplane

1 teaspoon chopped fresh parsley

¼ teaspoon kosher salt

FOR THE PIGS IN A BLANKET

1 (8-ounce/226 g) tube crescent roll dough

1 cup shredded mozzarella cheese

4 hot dogs

1 egg, beaten

Sesame seeds, for sprinkling

FOR SERVING

Marinara sauce, warmed

Savannah's main food group is finger food—and there is no better grub to grab than pigs in a blanket. "I'm very disappointed when I go to a party and there aren't pigs in a blanket," she says. "It's an absolute must." And while the plain ol' version is already a "perfect food" in her eyes, here she combines it with another finger-food phenom—garlic bread— to create something even more heavenly. Dunk it in marinara, if you desire, but, as Savannah says, "It's so good, it doesn't need to be dipped."

Make the garlic butter: In a small bowl, beat the butter, garlic, parsley, and salt until well combined. Set aside.

Make the pigs in a blanket: Preheat the oven to 375°F (190°C). Line a sheet pan with parchment paper.

On a clean work surface, unroll the dough. Lay 2 triangles of crescent roll dough next to each other, gently pinching them together to seal, to create a rectangle. Repeat to make a total of 4 rectangles.

Spread a heaping tablespoon of the garlic butter onto each dough rectangle, spreading it evenly across the surface. Sprinkle ¼ cup of the mozzarella evenly over each square. Place a hot dog along the longer end of each rectangle and roll it up to enclose, pinching the seam with your fingers to seal.

Cut each roll-up into 4 pieces and arrange on the lined sheet pan seam side down. Brush with the beaten egg and top with a sprinkling of sesame seeds.

Bake until golden brown and warmed through, 8 to 10 minutes.

Serve with marinara sauce.

Michael Symon's
EXTRA-HERBY SPANAKOPITA

MAKES 15 LARGE TRIANGLES
PREP TIME: 40 MINUTES
COOK TIME: 15 MINUTES
INACTIVE TIME: 30 MINUTES

FOR THE FILLING

4 tablespoons extra-virgin olive oil

3 (10-ounce/280 g) containers baby spinach

Kosher salt

2 scallions, thinly sliced

2 cloves garlic, minced

¼ cup (12 g) finely chopped fresh parsley

¼ cup (10 g) finely chopped fresh dill

2 (6-ounce/170 g) containers crumbled Greek feta cheese

1 large egg, beaten

¼ teaspoon freshly grated nutmeg

FOR ASSEMBLY

1 (16-ounce/455 g) box phyllo dough, preferably Athens brand

3 sticks (12 ounces/340 g) unsalted butter, melted

 TIPS

Keep the phyllo covered with a barely damp towel while working with it so it doesn't dry out.

If not using Athens brand phyllo dough, cut the sheets into 8½ by 13½-inch (20 by 34 cm) rectangles. You will need to use 2 boxes to have enough sheets.

Michael has been making spanakopita with his mom since before he could reach the kitchen counter. They'd stuff and fold the phyllo like little parcels containing the most delicious love notes, handing them out on a big tray to family members at every holiday. Though the chef and restaurateur stays mostly faithful to his mom's tried-and-true recipe, he freshens it up a bit with a hefty handful of herbs. The Greek know how to get their greens—and now you do, too.

Make the filling: In a large deep skillet, warm 3 tablespoons of the olive oil over medium-high heat. Add as much of the spinach as you can and begin to sweat, stirring constantly until it begins to wilt. Continue adding the spinach in batches and cook, stirring constantly, until softened and wilted, 9 to 11 minutes. Season with 1 teaspoon kosher salt and stir to combine. Transfer to a fine-mesh sieve set over a bowl and let sit for 30 minutes.

Transfer the spinach to the center of a clean kitchen towel and wring out as much excess moisture as possible. Roughly chop and transfer to a large bowl.

Add the scallions, garlic, parsley, dill, feta, egg, and remaining 1 tablespoon olive oil and mix well to combine. Season with salt to taste.

To assemble: Preheat the oven to 400°F (200°C).

Lay out one sheet of the phyllo and brush it with the melted butter. Layer another sheet on top and brush it with melted butter. Fold the phyllo in half lengthwise, then brush with melted butter (see Tip).

Set the folded phyllo with a short side facing you. Scoop ¼ cup (55 g) of the filling and place it on the side of the phyllo closest to you. Begin shaping the phyllo into a triangle, folding it over itself, and continue folding, like folding a flag, brushing with butter between each fold, until completely folded. Secure the seam with a light brushing of the butter and place the phyllo, seam side down, onto a sheet pan. Repeat with the remaining ingredients.

Bake until golden brown and crisp, 15 to 20 minutes. Serve warm.

Savannah's
CHEESE PLATE GUIDE

"I am somebody who can't cook but likes to entertain," says Savannah. "Putting things on a board is something I can do in the kitchen." She much prefers to socialize over snacks from 4 to 6 p.m.—with a cocktail, of course—over sitting down to a big meal from 6 to 8 p.m.

When it comes to her spread, she likes to experiment with different cheeses, crackers, and dips, but generally gets one or two things from each of these categories:

SOFT CHEESES

Double creme Brie

Goat cheese log

SEMI-SOFT CHEESES

Mild blue

Drunken goat

HARD CHEESES

Aged Gouda

Moliterno al tartufo

Parmigiano-Reggiano

Gruyère

Sharp white cheddar

Gouda

CRACKERS

Cranberry-almond crisps

Taralli

Breadsticks

Sea salt crackers

CONDIMENTS

Fig jam

Apricot jam

Gorgeous Green Dip
(recipe follows)

SNACKS

Castelvetrano olives

Marinated olives

Cornichons

Marcona almonds

Spiced pecans

"I am very big on preslicing the cheese," says Savannah. "At least get it started. It's a friendly thing to do."

AYESHA NURDJAJA'S GORGEOUS GREEN DIP

MAKES 4 CUPS

1 bunch cilantro

1 serrano chile, stemmed and roughly chopped

1½ teaspoons Dijon mustard

2 large egg yolks

1 large egg

5 small cloves garlic, peeled but whole

1½ teaspoons ground cumin

2 teaspoons kosher salt, plus more as needed

2 cups (240 ml) canola oil

¼ cup (60 ml) fresh lime juice, plus more to taste

This is the type of dip Savannah likes to put out with her cheese plate for an eye-catching pop of green in an otherwise rather beige spread. With bright and lively ingredients like cilantro, serrano chile, Dijon, garlic, and lime, it's the life of the party. Plus, it's very versatile: It can be used as a topping for grilled meat or seafood. If you'd like to use it as a dressing for vegetables and greens, add a bit more water and lime juice. If you'd like to use it as a sandwich spread, omit the water completely.

Trim the rough ends of the cilantro and discard, then roughly chop the leaves and stems and add them to a blender.

Add the serrano, mustard, egg yolks, whole egg, cumin, salt, and ¼ cup (60 ml) of the oil and blend, scraping down the sides of the blender pitcher as needed, until smooth.

With the machine running, add the remaining 1¾ cups (180 ml) of the oil in a slow, steady stream, processing until emulsified and thickened.

Add the lime juice and ¼ cup (60 ml) water in two additions, blending until fully emulsified. Season with salt and additional lime juice, to taste, if necessary.

Emi Boscamp's
TANGY TOMATO TART

SERVES 6 TO 8
PREP TIME: 25 MINUTES
COOK TIME: 35 MINUTES
INACTIVE TIME: 2 HOURS
    5 MINUTES (DOUGH RESTING,
    PLUS COOLING TIME)

FOR THE PASTRY DOUGH

2½ cups plus 2 tablespoons (315 g) all-purpose flour, plus more for dusting

½ teaspoon kosher salt

2 sticks (8 ounces/225 g) unsalted butter, cold, cut into ½-inch (13 mm) cubes

1 large egg, lightly beaten

3 to 4 tablespoons (45 to 60 ml) ice water

FOR THE FILLING

½ cup (130 g) Dijon mustard

1½ cups (170 grams) shredded Gruyère cheese

4 large heirloom tomatoes (about 1 pound/455 g each), cored and cut into slices ⅓ inch (1 cm) thick

Handful of cherry tomatoes, halved

Ingredients continue

 TIPS

Choose tomatoes in a variety of sizes for a funky visual effect, and don't worry if the crust isn't perfect—it's supposed to be rustic!

If you don't have a food processor, you can use a pastry cutter to make the dough.

Our senior food editor Emi's parents first tried tomato pie in 1988 on a trip to Anguilla. They were at a restaurant called Le Fish Trap, known across the island for its savory pastry painted with Dijon mustard, sprinkled with cheese, and topped with heirloom tomatoes. A few years later, while going through a pile of old magazines, her mom, Yuki, was shocked to spot the pie on the cover of *Gourmet* magazine. Emi's family has been making this tart every summer ever since. Over the years, they've adapted it in various ways, like doubling its size to fit on a half-sheet pan so there's more to go around.

Make the pastry dough: In a food processor, pulse the flour, salt, and butter until it has a mealy consistency. Add the egg, turn on the machine, and add the ice water, 1 tablespoon at a time, until the dough comes together, 3 to 4 tablespoons.

Turn the dough out onto a floured work surface and knead quickly, just to bring the dough together. Do not overwork the dough. Form the dough into a rectangle, wrap tightly in plastic wrap, and refrigerate for at least 1 hour and up to overnight.

Preheat the oven to 400°F (200°C).

Remove the dough from the refrigerator and let sit at room temperature until it is slightly pliable, 5 to 10 minutes.

On a lightly floured work surface, roll out the dough into a rectangle slightly larger than an 18 by 13-inch (45 by 33 cm) sheet pan. Transfer the dough to the sheet pan, gently pressing it into the corners.

Add the filling: Using a pastry brush, spread the mustard evenly over the bottom of the pastry dough. Sprinkle the Gruyère evenly over the mustard. Arrange the tomatoes over the cheese in a colorful pattern, touching but not overlapping; they should cover the whole surface. Fill in any gaps with the cherry tomatoes.

Recipe continues

FOR THE HERB OIL

¼ cup (15 g) finely chopped fresh parsley

2 tablespoons finely chopped fresh oregano

4 cloves garlic, minced

⅓ cup (80 ml) extra-virgin olive oil

Flaky sea salt, for serving

Bake until the pastry is golden brown and the cheese is bubbling and starting to brown, 30 to 40 minutes.

Meanwhile, make the herb oil: In a small bowl, mix together the parsley, oregano, garlic, and oil to combine.

When the tart comes out of the oven, drizzle evenly with the herb oil. Allow the tart to cool to room temperature before serving.

Slice into squares and serve with a sprinkling of flaky sea salt.

Green Room:
SALADS & SOUPS

This is where we relax between segments, where we find refuge from the chaos of live TV. These recipes (with the exception of Craig's chili) provide the lightness and brightness you may seek with some of the heartier ones in the book. We considered making this the lunch chapter, but the scope of soups and salads extends beyond lunchtime. They refresh us, comfort us, and, in many cases, stand alone as their own meal (see the Cobb Salad, page 82, or Chorizo Clam Chowder, page 89)—whether that's in the afternoon or evening.

Hoda's
UPSIDE-DOWN SALAD

SERVES 6
PREP TIME: 15 MINUTES

FOR THE BALSAMIC DRESSING

½ cup (120 ml) extra-virgin olive oil

⅓ cup (80 ml) balsamic vinegar

1 large clove garlic, grated on a Microplane

1 teaspoon honey

¼ teaspoon Dijon mustard

¼ teaspoon kosher salt

¼ teaspoon freshly ground black pepper

FOR THE SALAD

2 avocados, diced

2 Champagne mangoes, diced

1 cup (150 g) cherry tomatoes, halved

½ English cucumber, sliced into half-moons

1 head iceberg lettuce, chopped into 1-inch (2.5 cm) pieces

1 cup (55 g) seasoned croutons

When Hoda was a kid, she and her siblings always had a job at dinnertime: One of them would set the table, another would be in charge of clearing the table, and someone else would make the salad. This is what Hoda would make when she was on salad duty. She'd build it from the bottom up: First, she'd make the vinaigrette and combine it in a salad bowl with avocado, mango, cucumber, and tomatoes, letting everything mingle. Then, when ready to serve, she'd toss it with the lettuce and croutons. And to this day, it's still Hoda's go-to salad. "It sounds really basic," she says, "but those mangoes tossed in the balsamic—it's like candy to me."

Make the balsamic dressing: In a screw-top jar, combine the olive oil, vinegar, garlic, honey, mustard, salt, and pepper, cover, and shake vigorously to emulsify.

Make the salad: In a large bowl, combine the avocados, mangoes, tomatoes, cucumber, and the dressing and toss to combine. Add the lettuce, then top with the croutons.

When ready to serve, toss the salad until all ingredients are evenly coated with the dressing.

Nancy Silverton's
PANZANELLA TOAST

SERVES 8
PREP TIME: 25 MINUTES
COOK TIME: 20 MINUTES

FOR THE VINAIGRETTE

¼ cup (60 ml) red wine vinegar

2 tablespoons dried oregano

1 tablespoon fresh lemon juice, or more to taste

1 large clove garlic, grated on a Microplane

½ teaspoon kosher salt, or more to taste

¼ teaspoon freshly ground black pepper, or more to taste

1 cup (240 ml) extra-virgin olive oil

FOR THE SALAD

1 (1-pound/455 g) loaf crusty white bread

4 tablespoons extra-virgin olive oil

3 large cloves garlic, peeled but whole

½ pint (170 g) Sungold tomatoes, halved

½ pint (170 g) heirloom cherry tomatoes, halved

1 tablespoon kosher salt

2 celery stalks, sliced into half-moons ¼ inch (6 mm) thick

1 small red onion, julienned

3 bell peppers in mixed colors, cut into ¼-inch (6 mm) strips

1 small fennel bulb, julienned

½ cup (80 g) small pitted black olives, such as Taggiasca or Niçoise, halved

¼ cup (50 g) capers

1 small handful small basil leaves, plus more for garnish

1 small handful mint leaves

1 small handful celery leaves, preferably pale green

The best kind of salad is a bread salad. Not a salad with bread, but a bread-based salad, with vegetables as supporting actors—aka panzanella. Nancy's take on the Tuscan staple features a rainbow of fresh ingredients—tomatoes, onions, celery, peppers, fennel, capers, olives, mint, and basil—and instead of tossing the bread into the salad, the chef and co-owner of the Mozza Restaurant Group uses it as the base. That thirsty loaf in your cupboard is begging to soak up the vinaigrette and tomato juices and become the star of your summer table.

Preheat the oven to 350°F (180°C).

Make the vinaigrette: In a medium bowl, whisk together the vinegar, oregano, lemon juice, garlic, salt, and pepper to combine. Add the oil in a slow thin stream, whisking constantly, until emulsified. Season with more salt, pepper, or lemon juice to taste.

Make the salad: Cut the bread into eight ¾-inch (2 cm) slices and arrange on a baking sheet. Brush the tops with 2 tablespoons of the olive oil and bake until golden brown and crisp, 15 to 20 minutes.

Immediately rub the bread with the garlic cloves.

Meanwhile, in a medium bowl, combine the tomatoes, remaining 2 tablespoons oil, and salt and use a slotted metal spoon to vigorously stir, without crushing them, until the juices release and emulsify with the oil.

In a large bowl, toss the celery, red onion, bell peppers, fennel, olives, capers, and ½ cup (120 ml) of the vinaigrette to combine. Add the basil, mint, and celery leaves and gently toss to combine.

To serve, place a slice of garlic toast onto each serving plate. Spoon the vegetable mixture evenly over the bread. Spoon the tomato mixture evenly over the vegetable mixture. Spoon some of the remaining vinaigrette over each salad, garnish with basil, and serve immediately.

Craig's Mom's
PIMENTO POTATO SALAD

SERVES 8
PREP TIME: 25 MINUTES
COOK TIME: 30 MINUTES
INACTIVE TIME: 1 HOUR

5 large russet potatoes (about 4 pounds/1.8 kg total), peeled and cut into ½-inch (13 mm) cubes

Kosher salt

1 cup (220 g) mayonnaise

½ cup (65 g) finely diced sweet onion

1 (4-ounce/113 g) jar sliced sweet pimentos, drained and roughly chopped

½ cup (130 g) sweet relish

4 large hard-boiled eggs, roughly chopped

1 tablespoon yellow mustard

1 teaspoon celery seed

1 teaspoon dried dillweed

Craig's mom, Betty Jo, always brought the potato salad to the family functions. "If someone new showed up with potato salad, we would tell them, 'Put it back in the car. Don't you come into this house offending our family,'" he says with a laugh. Her Southern-style potato salad is creamy thanks to mayonnaise and hard-boiled eggs, tangy thanks to relish and mustard, and a little sweet thanks to chopped pimentos. It will be a welcome addition to any cookout you're attending—just make sure someone else's mom isn't already in charge of making it.

In a large soup pot, combine the potatoes, a generous handful of salt, and enough cold water to cover by 1 inch (2.5 cm). Bring to a rolling boil over high heat and cook until very fork-tender, about 30 minutes.

Drain the potatoes, transfer to a bowl, and refrigerate until completely chilled, about 1 hour.

Add the mayonnaise, onion, pimentos, relish, hard-boiled eggs, mustard, celery seed, dried dill, and ½ teaspoon kosher salt and gently toss to combine.

Camila Alves McConaughey's
NO-MAYO COLESLAW

SERVES 6
PREP TIME: 20 MINUTES

2 tablespoons fresh lemon juice

2 tablespoons extra-virgin olive oil

2 teaspoons apple cider vinegar

1 teaspoon white wine vinegar

1 teaspoon kosher salt

1 small head green cabbage, cored and very finely shredded

1 large Granny Smith apple, julienned

½ small red onion, julienned

3 tablespoons coarsely chopped fresh mint

"I have never been a fan of coleslaw," says Women of Today founder Camila. The idea of creamy, soggy cabbage never appealed to her. So, she created this no-mayo version that is crisp and vibrant, thanks to fresh ingredients and plenty of acid. This slaw is her secret weapon for perking up any summery spread—think barbecue, fish, tacos, burgers, or Elizabeth Heiskell's Kickin' Fried Chicken (page 153). And, unlike its mayo-based cousin, it won't go sad and limp after a little too long in the sun.

In a large bowl, whisk together the lemon juice, olive oil, apple cider vinegar, white wine vinegar, and salt to combine. Add the cabbage, apple, red onion, and mint and toss, making sure all ingredients are evenly coated.

MAKE AHEAD

This dish actually benefits from a night in the fridge, as the flavors will have more time to meld. If making ahead, feel free to adjust the seasoning by adding a splash of oil and/or white wine vinegar and a pinch of salt.

Hillary Sterling's

ROASTED BEETS WITH FIERY ROMESCO

SERVES 6
PREP TIME: 30 MINUTES
COOK TIME: 1 HOUR
INACTIVE TIME: 30 MINUTES

FOR THE BEETS

3 bunches baby beets (about 1 pound/455 g total), cleaned, dried, and tops removed

2 tablespoons extra-virgin olive oil

1½ teaspoons kosher salt

FOR THE MARINADE

Juice of 3 large navel oranges

1 cup (240 ml) extra-virgin olive oil

½ cup (120 ml) red wine vinegar

Kosher salt

FOR THE GARLIC CONFIT AND OIL

1 head garlic, cloves separated and peeled

½ cup (120 ml) extra-virgin olive oil

FOR THE ROMESCO

1 medium red bell pepper

¼ cup (40 g) raw almonds

½ cup (120 ml) red wine vinegar

¾ cup (105 g) Marcona almonds, chopped

2 whole roasted red peppers from a jar, seeded

2 tablespoons crushed Calabrian chile peppers

Hillary, chef at Ci Siamo in New York City, transforms the humble beet into a remarkable root vegetable using a punchy marinade and a bold sauce. Orange juice and red wine vinegar brighten them up, while the sweet pepper and almond sauce—reminiscent of a romesco but with a bit more heat— adds complexity and texture. Don't forget to peel your beets while they're still warm: Rub them with a kitchen towel (that you don't mind staining) and the skins should fall right off.

Preheat the oven to 375°F (190°C).

Roast the beets: In a large bowl, toss together the beets, oil, and salt until the beets are evenly coated. Place the beets in a roasting pan, add 1 inch (2.5 cm) of water and cover tightly with foil. Roast until fork-tender, about 30 minutes.

Meanwhile, make the marinade: In a large bowl, whisk together the orange juice, olive oil, and red wine vinegar to combine. Season with salt to taste.

When cool enough to handle, but still warm, using a clean kitchen towel, rub the beets to remove the skin. Halve the beets and add them to the marinade. Let sit for 30 minutes.

Meanwhile, make the garlic confit: In a small saucepan, cook the garlic and oil over very low heat for 30 minutes. Measure out ¼ cup (60 ml) of the garlic oil for the romesco sauce.

Make the romesco: In a food processor, combine the bell peppers, raw almonds, confit garlic cloves, garlic oil, vinegar, ½ cup (70 g) of the Marcona almonds, the roasted red peppers, and Calabrian chiles and pulse until coarsely chopped.

To serve, add a large spoonful of the sauce to a serving plate, then top with the beets and the reserved Marcona almonds.

Katie Lee Biegel's
CHOPPED DILL PICKLE SALAD

SERVES 8
PREP TIME: 20 MINUTES
COOK TIME: 5 MINUTES

FOR THE DRESSING

1 cup (240 ml) mayonnaise

½ cup (130 ml) plain yogurt

¼ cup (60 ml) buttermilk, well-shaken

2 tablespoons minced fresh chives

2 tablespoons minced fresh flat-leaf parsley

½ teaspoon dried dill

2 tablespoons dill pickle juice

1 tablespoon distilled white vinegar

¼ teaspoon kosher salt

¼ teaspoon freshly ground black pepper

¼ teaspoon garlic powder

FOR THE BREAD CRUMBS

1 tablespoon unsalted butter

1 tablespoon extra-virgin olive oil

1 cup (80 g) panko bread crumbs

¼ teaspoon kosher salt

FOR THE SALAD

3 large curly kale leaves, stemmed and finely chopped

1 head romaine, cored and finely chopped

½ small head red cabbage, thinly sliced

½ small head cauliflower, finely chopped

1 large handful fresh dill, roughly chopped

½ (15-ounce/425 g) can chickpeas, drained and rinsed

3 radishes, thinly sliced

3 small dill pickles, chopped

Katie, cohost of *The Kitchen*, is "legitimately dill pickle obsessed" (she loves a pickle martini), and her favorite meal is "a big salad." So, she realized, she had to combine the two—and this salad was born. We can't get enough of the creamy dill dressing, the crunchy kale-cabbage-cauliflower mixture, the chopped pickles, of course, and the pièce de résistance: the toasted bread crumbs. Why not croutons, you ask? Toasted bread crumbs take the win because they accomplish more crunch coverage. "This salad really has it all," she says.

Make the dressing: In a medium bowl, mix together the mayonnaise, yogurt, buttermilk, chives, parsley, dried dill, pickle juice, vinegar, salt, pepper, and garlic powder until well combined. Set aside.

Make the bread crumbs: In a nonstick medium skillet, melt the butter in the oil over medium heat. Add the panko, season with the salt, and cook, stirring constantly, until golden brown, 2 to 4 minutes. Transfer to a bowl and cool completely.

Make the salad: In a large bowl, toss together the kale, romaine, cabbage, cauliflower, fresh dill, chickpeas, radishes, and pickles to combine. Drizzle the dressing around the rim of the bowl, then toss until all ingredients are evenly coated.

Sprinkle the bread crumbs over the top and serve.

MAKE AHEAD

You can store the dressing in the refrigerator for up to 1 week—and use it to marinate chicken, as a dipping sauce for crudités, a condiment for sandwiches, or a dressing for any other type of salad (potato, pasta, egg, tuna, chicken, and more).

Alex Guarnaschelli's
WEDGE-STYLE COBB SALAD

SERVES 4
PREP TIME: 25 MINUTES
COOK TIME: 45 MINUTES

FOR THE DRESSING

9 tablespoons (135 ml) extra-virgin olive oil

6 tablespoons (90 ml) apple cider vinegar

2 tablespoons Dijon mustard

2 teaspoons dried oregano

1 medium shallot, minced

FOR THE SALAD

4 large eggs

Kosher salt

8 slices bacon, cut into 1-inch (2.5 cm) strips

4 bone-in, skin-on chicken thighs (about 2 pounds/910 g total)

1 pint (10 ounces/285 g) cherry tomatoes, halved

1 teaspoon sugar

2 medium heads iceberg lettuce, ends trimmed and each halved to create 4 iceberg "rounds"

2 medium avocados, cut into ½-inch (13 mm) cubes

6 ounces (170 g) crumbled blue cheese

Freshly ground black pepper

 TIP

Season each component individually so that when the salads are assembled, the flavor is evenly distributed.

Alex used to make a version of this Cobb salad every day, decades ago, when she first started her culinary career at chef Larry Forgione's restaurant An American Place, which was just a short walk from 30 Rock, home of TODAY. The Cobb implies a promise of bacon, chicken, blue cheese, and avocado on lettuce—and nothing fancy when it comes to lettuce. The chef and host of *Ciao House* uses iceberg "rounds" as crunchy serving vessels, which gives it a wedge-like feel. Carve yourself a bite with everything in it and you'll be transported to Midtown Manhattan in the '90s on your lunch break.

Preheat the oven to 350°F (180°C).

Make the dressing: In a medium bowl, whisk together the olive oil, vinegar, mustard, oregano, shallot, and 1 tablespoon water until fully emulsified.

Make the salad: Gently place the eggs in a medium pot, cover them with cold water, and add a pinch of salt. Bring to a rolling boil over high heat, then remove from the heat, cover, and let sit for 10 minutes.

Carefully pour off the hot water and then run cool water over the eggs until cool enough to handle. Gently crack the eggs and peel, rinsing them off with cold water, as needed.

Halve the eggs, lengthwise, then cut in half again to create quarter egg wedges. Season with salt and set aside.

Line a plate with paper towels and have near the stove. In a large ovenproof skillet, sauté the bacon over medium heat until crispy, 8 to 12 minutes. Transfer the bacon to the paper towels, leaving the rendered fat in the pan.

Recipe continues

Season the chicken on both sides with salt. Place the chicken, skin side down, into the skillet and cook over medium heat until browned, about 6 minutes.

Using tongs, flip the chicken, place the skillet into the oven, and roast the chicken until it is cooked through and registers 165°F (75°C) on an instant thermometer, about 20 minutes.

Transfer the chicken to a cutting board and let rest while you assemble the salad.

In a small bowl, gently stir the tomatoes and sugar to combine and set aside.

Place a lettuce round on each plate, cutting each into four pieces like you would a pizza and put them back together as if they are still whole. Season with a sprinkle of salt and add a generous spoonful of the dressing and some of the pan drippings over the top.

Remove the chicken from the bones and cut into bite-sized pieces.

Scatter the avocados, tomatoes, egg wedges, blue cheese, bacon, and chicken over the salad. Drizzle evenly with the remaining dressing and season with a couple of turns of freshly ground black pepper. Serve immediately.

Alejandra Ramos's
SPICY CHORIZO CLAM CHOWDER

**SERVES 6 AS AN APPETIZER,
OR 4 AS A MAIN COURSE
PREP TIME: 20 MINUTES
COOK TIME: 50 MINUTES**

4 pounds (1.8 kg) clams, such as Manila or littleneck, scrubbed under cold running water

5¼ ounces (150 g) Spanish-style chorizo, diced

2 slices thick-cut bacon, diced

2 celery stalks, sliced

1 medium yellow onion, diced

2 large cloves garlic, minced

2 teaspoons smoked paprika

2 large russet potatoes, peeled and diced

1½ cups (360 ml) whole milk

1 cup (240 ml) heavy cream

Kosher salt and freshly ground black pepper

Oyster crackers, for serving

Chopped fresh parsley and/or scallions, for garnish

If there's one food Alejandra, host of *The Great American Recipe*, couldn't live without, it's Spanish chorizo. She puts it into almost everything she cooks—not as the main ingredient, but more as a condiment—allowing the pimentón-seasoned sausage to lend dishes its spicy, smoky flavor and vibrant crimson color. It plays a particularly exciting supporting role in this clam chowder, where its flavor cuts right through the richness of the dairy. Unlike its much heavier New England cousin, this soup skips the roux-thickened base in favor of a light yet boldly flavored broth that really lets the briny clams shine.

Place the clams in a medium saucepan, add 2 cups (480 ml) cold water, cover, set over medium-high heat and let steam until the clams begin to open, about 8 minutes. Remove the clams as they open, keeping the saucepan covered in between, until all the clams have opened. Discard any clams that do not open.

Line a sieve with cheesecloth and set over a bowl. Pour the clam cooking liquid into the sieve. Discard the solids and reserve the liquid. Remove the clams from their shells, placing them in a bowl and cover with a damp paper towel.

In a large heavy-bottomed pot, sauté the chorizo and bacon over medium heat, stirring periodically, until the bacon is rendered and the chorizo is lightly crisp, 5 to 7 minutes. Using a slotted spoon, transfer the bacon and chorizo to a bowl, leaving the rendered fat behind.

Add the celery, onions, garlic, and smoked paprika to the fat in the pan and sauté until slightly softened, 2 to 3 minutes. Add the reserved clam liquid, 1½ cups (360 ml) water, and the potatoes and cook until the potatoes are tender, 10 to 15 minutes.

Recipe continues

Add the milk, cream, and chorizo/bacon mixture and gently simmer, reducing the heat as needed, for 10 minutes.

Add the clams, stir to combine, and simmer for an additional 5 minutes. Season with salt and pepper to taste.

Serve with oyster crackers and garnish with parsley and/or scallions before serving.

 TIPS

The trick when cooking with clams is to keep cooking time to a minimum. For this chowder, lightly steam the clams, remove them from their shells, and set them aside. Then wait until just before serving to add them to the soup.

If you anticipate having leftovers and want to be able to reheat the chowder without overcooking the clams, keep them stored in the fridge in a separate container, only adding a few to each bowl just before serving; the heat from the steaming broth will be just enough to heat them through without affecting that perfect, chewy bite.

Lazarus Lynch's
COCONUT CURRY CARROT SOUP

SERVES 4
PREP TIME: 30 MINUTES
COOK TIME: 50 MINUTES

FOR THE ROASTED VEGETABLES

1 pound (455 g) carrots, rinsed, trimmed and chopped into large pieces

½ Granny Smith apple, peeled

1 small yellow onion, chopped

1 orange bell pepper, large diced

½ habanero pepper, stemmed and seeded

2 cloves garlic, peeled but whole

1 teaspoon grated fresh ginger

2 teaspoons curry powder

1 teaspoon fresh thyme leaves

½ teaspoon each ground allspice, cardamom, and cinnamon

2 teaspoons kosher salt

1 teaspoon freshly ground black pepper

¼ cup (60 ml) extra-virgin olive oil

FOR THE APPLE SALSA

½ cup finely chopped peeled Granny Smith apple

¼ cup (30 g) finely chopped jicama

½ cup (80 g) fresh pomegranate seeds

2 teaspoons chopped fresh parsley

Splash of rice wine vinegar

Pinch of kosher salt

FOR THE SOUP

1 (13.5-ounce/400 ml) can unsweetened full-fat coconut milk

½ cup (120 ml) vegetable broth

Kosher salt and freshly ground black pepper

When he's seeking comfort after a stressful day, Lazarus, author of *Son of a Southern Chef*, turns to this nourishing recipe. Carrots may not be the most exciting vegetable, but roasting them brings out their natural sweetness, and blending them gives them a smooth and velvety texture—ideal for soup. Seasoned with Caribbean flavors, this dish gets a little kick from the habanero, while the coconut milk cools it down. It may seem fitting for fall—and it is!—but it should be enjoyed whenever your soul needs soothing, no matter the time of year.

Preheat the oven to 400°F (200°C).

Roast the vegetables: In a large bowl, toss together the carrots, apple, onion, bell pepper, habanero, garlic, ginger, curry powder, thyme, allspice, cardamom, cinnamon, salt, black pepper, and oil.

Spread the mixture onto a large sheet pan and roast until tender and caramelized, about 40 minutes.

Meanwhile, make the apple salsa: In a medium bowl, mix together the apple, jicama, pomegranate, parsley, vinegar, and salt to combine. Set aside.

Finish the soup: Transfer the roasted vegetables to a blender, add the coconut milk and vegetable broth and blend until smooth.

Transfer to a saucepan and warm over medium heat. Season with salt and pepper to taste.

Ladle the soup into serving bowls and top with some apple salsa. Serve immediately.

 TIP

If you have any of José Andrés's Cumin-Roasted Carrots (page 96) left over, turn them into this dish!

Alison Roman's
DILLY BEAN STEW WITH CABBAGE & FRIZZLED ONIONS

SERVES 4
PREP TIME: 15 MINUTES
COOK TIME: 40 MINUTES

2 tablespoons unsalted butter

2 tablespoons extra-virgin olive oil, plus more for drizzling

1 large yellow onion, thinly sliced

Kosher salt and freshly ground black pepper

2 (15.5-ounce/439 g) cans white beans such as navy, butter, cannellini, drained and rinsed

4 cups (960 ml) vegetable or chicken broth

¼ head green cabbage (about 8 ounces/225 g), cored and coarsely chopped

1 tablespoon distilled white vinegar

1 cup (40 g) coarsely chopped fresh dill

Sour cream (optional)

 TIPS

While most white beans work great here, mixing a few types will get you the best variety of creaminess, texture, and flavor (Alison prefers the combo of tiny navy beans and large butter beans.)

When cooking the frizzled onions, you do not want jammy, caramelized onions, but you also do not want burnt onions, so just adjust the heat and frequency of stirring as needed.

"This stew doesn't look like much," cookbook author Alison says, **"but we all know it's not what the ingredients are—it's how they're treated."** The onions must be frizzled (somewhere between caramelized and fried), the beans must be cooked and lightly crushed before any liquid is added (or your stew will be a soup), the dill must not be skimped on (hence the "dilly" descriptor), and the vinegar must be used (to wake up the entire dish from its stew-y slumber). Add a dollop of sour cream at the end if you're a sucker for sour cream and onion chips.

In a large saucepan, warm the butter and oil over medium-high heat. Add the onion and a generous pinch of salt and pepper and cook, without stirring too much or too frequently, until the onions are nicely browned and frizzled, 5 to 8 minutes.

Using a slotted spoon, transfer one-quarter of the onions to a small bowl. Set aside.

Add the beans and a generous pinch of salt and some pepper to the pan and use a wooden spoon to break up some of the beans to release their creaminess and starchiness. Add the broth, bring to a simmer, and cook, stirring occasionally, until the texture turns stew-y, 15 to 20 minutes.

Add the cabbage and vinegar, stirring to wilt. Continue simmering until the cabbage is totally tender and the flavors have melded, 10 to 15 minutes.

Season with salt and pepper to taste. Remove from the heat and stir in half of the dill.

Divide the stew among bowls and top with the remaining dill, the reserved frizzled onions, a drizzle of olive oil, a crack of black pepper, and a dollop of sour cream (if using). Serve immediately.

Craig's
SUPERCHARGED CHILI

SERVES 4
PREP TIME: 15 MINUTES
COOK TIME: 45 MINUTES

1 tablespoon olive oil

1 pound (455 g) ground beef (80/20)

½ pound (225 g) loose pork sausage, such as Jimmy Dean

1 medium yellow onion, finely diced

1 medium green bell pepper, finely diced

1 tablespoon minced garlic

1 tablespoon chili powder

2 teaspoons adobo seasoning

1 teaspoon ground cumin

1 teaspoon kosher salt

½ teaspoon freshly ground black pepper

1 (28-ounce/795 g) can crushed tomatoes

1 (15-ounce/425 g) can three-bean blend, drained and rinsed

½ teaspoon instant espresso powder

FOR SERVING

Shredded cheddar cheese

Sliced jalapeños

Sour cream

"This is a staple for my family during the winter," says Craig. **"It's one of the few dishes that my kids will eat reliably."** Not just any chili recipe, his is packed with a combo of beef, pork sausage, and beans (sorry, Texans!), and its secret ingredient is instant espresso, which adds "a little depth of flavor," he says. Its bitterness cuts through the fattiness of the meat, adds an earthy richness, and amplifies the smoky spices, making for a full-bodied bowl of comfort.

In a Dutch oven, warm the oil over medium-high heat. Add the beef and sausage and sauté, breaking the meat into small pieces with a wooden spoon, until browned, about 5 minutes. Using a slotted spoon, transfer the meat to a plate, leaving the pan drippings behind.

Add the onion and bell pepper and cook, stirring often, until softened, about 5 minutes.

Add the garlic and cook, stirring often, for 1 minute. Add the chili powder, adobo seasoning, cumin, salt, and black pepper and toast, stirring constantly, for 30 seconds. Stir in the crushed tomatoes and the browned meat and bring to a simmer. Reduce the heat to medium-low, cover, and cook, stirring periodically, for 30 minutes.

Add the beans and espresso powder, stir to combine, and cook, uncovered, stirring occasionally, for 5 minutes.

To serve: Ladle into bowls and top with cheddar cheese, sliced jalapeños and a dollop of sour cream. Serve immediately.

Special Guests:
SIDES

Just as guests bring the excitement to our show, side dishes bring the same energy to the table. They are the real stars, especially when it comes to the holidays. Don't get us wrong—we love a show-stopping roast—but it would be nothing without its supporting cast of sides. This is where you will find the bulk of the vegetables, from Sheinelle's collard greens to Hoda's burnt broccoli, and starchy casseroles, from Craig's mac and cheese to Al's sweet potato poon (because of course we had to include that).

José Andrés's
CUMIN-ROASTED CARROTS

SERVES 4
PREP TIME: 15 MINUTES
COOK TIME: 10 MINUTES

Kosher salt

2 bunches rainbow carrots, thoroughly washed and tops trimmed

¾ teaspoon cumin seeds

1 clove garlic, peeled but whole

¼ cup (60 ml) extra-virgin olive oil

2 tablespoons sherry vinegar, preferably Spanish

Freshly ground black pepper

Carrots with cumin (zanahorias con comino) is a classic tapa found throughout the south of Spain, in Andalusia, but its origins can be traced across the Mediterranean—to Morocco. It's a simple recipe, to be sure, but each step is important. Toasting the cumin seeds adds a layer of complexity—don't use ground cumin here, or you will miss out!—and grinding the seeds with garlic to create a paste makes for an intensely flavorful dressing. José prefers to make this dish when carrots are in season. "Yes, you can find carrots all year long," says the founder of the José Andrés Group, "but I like to get the sweetest carrots from my local farmers' market in spring and fall." He keeps the carrots whole when serving them, but you can also slice them into rounds before tossing in the dressing.

Bring a large soup pot of generously salted water to a rolling boil.

Add the carrots and cook until tender but still firm, about 7 minutes. Reserve 3 tablespoons of the cooking liquid and drain the carrots.

Using a clean kitchen towel, carefully rub the carrots to remove any rough skin, leaving a smooth surface. Set aside.

In a small sauté pan, toast the cumin over medium heat until fragrant, about 1 minute.

Transfer the cumin to a mortar, add ¼ teaspoon salt and the garlic, and use the pestle to grind the ingredients to form a paste. Transfer to a large bowl. Add the oil and vinegar and whisk to emulsify. Add the reserved cooking liquid and whisk until completely combined.

Add the carrots and toss until evenly coated with the dressing. Season with salt and pepper to taste and serve warm or at room temperature.

Craig's Mom's
OVER-THE-TOP
MAC & CHEESE

SERVES 12
PREP TIME: 10 MINUTES
COOK TIME: 55 MINUTES
INACTIVE TIME: 10 MINUTES

Softened butter, for the baking pan

Salt

1 pound (455 g) elbow macaroni

1 stick (4 ounces/115 g) salted butter, cubed, at room temperature

1 (12-ounce/354 ml) can evaporated milk

1 cup (240 ml) whole milk

3 large eggs, beaten

1 (8-ounce/225 g) block processed cheese product, such as Velveeta, broken up into small chunks

2 cups shredded sharp cheddar cheese (8 ounces/225 g)

2 cups shredded mild cheddar cheese (8 ounces/225 g)

Kosher salt and freshly ground black pepper

"This is the official side dish of our family," says Craig. **"It's the stuff of legend."** Let us be crystal clear: This recipe is not healthy. It's probably about 5,000 calories a serving (don't quote us on that). It uses two forms of milk, three different types of cheese (if you consider Velveeta a cheese), and a whole lotta butter. Needless to say, it's the first dish to go at Thanksgiving—or any gathering. Craig's mom, Betty Jo, says eggs are the "secret ingredient" that holds everything together and makes this super-comforting dish somehow even more comforting.

Preheat the oven to 425°F (218°C). Grease a 9 by 13-inch (23 by 33 cm) baking pan with butter.

Bring a large pot of salted water to a boil. Add the macaroni and cook to al dente according to the package directions.

Drain the elbows and transfer to a large bowl. Add the butter and stir until the butter is completely melted and the elbows are evenly coated. Add the evaporated milk, whole milk, and eggs and stir until well combined. Add the Velveeta, 1½ cups (170 g) of the sharp cheddar, and 1½ cups (170 g) of the mild cheddar and mix to combine. Season with salt and pepper to taste.

Pour the mixture into the prepared baking pan. Sprinkle the remaining ½ cup (55 g) of sharp cheddar and ½ cup (55 g) of mild cheddar evenly over the top.

Bake until the cheese is crispy and deep golden brown and bubbling around the edges, about 45 minutes.

Let rest for 10 minutes before serving.

Sheinelle's
KICKED-UP COLLARD GREENS

SERVES 12
PREP TIME: 15 MINUTES
COOK TIME: 2 HOURS

1 (8-ounce/225 g) jar chicken base, such as Better Than Bouillon Roasted Chicken Base

1 (10-ounce/283 g) can diced tomatoes and green chilies, such as Ro-tel

2 smoked turkey drumsticks

1 large white onion, diced

1 large jalapeño, seeded, deribbed, and finely diced

2 dried cayenne peppers

1 teaspoon freshly ground black pepper

1 tablespoon distilled white vinegar

4 pounds (1.8 kg) collard greens, washed and patted dry

Sea salt

Everybody has a go-to dish they bring to a potluck. For Sheinelle, that's her spicy collard greens—a recipe passed down from her grandmother. The key ingredient, she insists, is the can of Ro-tel tomatoes and green chilies, which adds a little kick. Her grandmother used to use smoked ham hocks, but now Sheinelle prefers the flavor imparted by smoked turkey. "It's always so tender and yummy, and it just feels good to eat," she says, and it'll go with everything else in the spread.

In a large soup pot, stir the chicken base into 3 quarts (2.8 L) water until dissolved. Add the diced tomatoes and green chilies, turkey drums, onion, jalapeño, cayenne peppers, black pepper, and vinegar. Bring to a boil, then reduce the heat to a simmer and cook until the meat is tender, about 15 minutes.

Meanwhile, on a large cutting board, stack several fully opened collard leaves and, with a chef's knife, remove the thick stem ends, the midribs, and any discolored leaves and discard. Cut the leaves, crosswise, into strips 2 inches (5 cm) wide.

Increase the heat under the pot to medium-high, add the collard greens, and cook, stirring often, until the greens have wilted, about 5 minutes. Reduce the heat to a simmer, cover, and cook, stirring occasionally, until the greens are very tender, about 1 hour 30 minutes.

Remove the turkey legs and transfer to a sheet pan to cool. Fish out the cayenne peppers and discard.

Return the pot to a boil over medium-high heat and cook uncovered for 5 to 10 minutes to reduce.

Meanwhile, shred the turkey meat into bite-sized pieces.

Add the turkey meat to the greens, season with sea salt to taste, and serve.

Carson's Mom's
CLOUD NINE MASHED POTATOES

SERVES 8
PREP TIME: 10 MINUTES
COOK TIME: 55 MINUTES

12 medium Yukon Gold potatoes (about 4 pounds/1.8 kg total), peeled

¼ cup (37 g) kosher salt, plus more, as needed

1 stick (4 ounces/115 g) unsalted butter, at room temperature, plus melted butter for serving

¼ cup (60 ml) gin or vodka

1⅔ cups (395 ml) half-and-half, warmed

Freshly ground black pepper

Optional toppings: crumbled bacon, roasted garlic, fried shallots, and chopped chives

Carson's late mom Pattie's mashed potatoes have a secret ingredient: gin. It's still up for debate in the Daly family whether its addition was intentional or not, but the fact is, the recipe makes super-smooth and creamy mashed potatoes that'll have you on cloud nine. Carson claims that "there is a method to the madness," saying that the alcohol keeps the dish from clumping. "It's not gratuitous, but it sure is fun."

Thoroughly rinse the potatoes, then place them in a large pot. Add enough cold water to cover the potatoes by 1 inch (2.5 cm), then add the salt. Bring to a boil over high heat. Reduce to a simmer and cook until the potatoes are very tender and easily pierced with a fork, about 35 minutes.

Drain the potatoes, return them to the pot, and let sit to allow any excess moisture evaporate, about 1 minute.

Add the butter, gin, and half-and-half and use a potato masher to mash to your desired level of creaminess. Season with salt and pepper to taste.

Serve immediately with a generous drizzling of melted butter and toppings of choice.

 TIP

Mash the potatoes by hand with a masher, or use a ricer—never use a food processor or blender, or you'll end up with a gluey mess!

Julius Roberts's
SPRING ASPARAGUS TUMBLE WITH BURRATA

SERVES 8
PREP TIME: 15 MINUTES
COOK TIME: 15 MINUTES
INACTIVE TIME: 5 MINUTES

2 leeks

2 tablespoons extra-virgin olive oil, plus more for drizzling

4 cloves garlic, thinly sliced

Flaky sea salt

1 bunch of asparagus, woody ends snapped off

Dry white wine

1 cup (150 g) frozen peas

Grated zest and juice of 1 organic lemon

Freshly ground black pepper

4 (4-ounce/115 g) balls burrata, at room temperature

Small bunch of fresh mint leaves, torn

Small bunch of fresh basil leaves, torn

 TIP

The key to this dish is timing. Make sure each ingredient is cooked to perfection by adding them in stages, seasoning and tasting as you go.

Asparagus just sings spring—and cook, author, and farmer Julius loves to braise it to keep it bright and juicy. Here, he does so with leeks, peas, and garlic, finishes it with mint, basil, and lemon, and tops it with burrata. The contrast of the warm, sweet tumble of green with the cold and creamy burrata is a delight for the senses. Paired with hunks of sourdough and some salami, it's the ideal lunch for a sunny day in spring. But you can divide the balls of burrata among three or four to serve it as a vibrant and zingy starter.

Trim off the green ends, almost all the way to the white, of the leeks. Discard. Cut the leeks crosswise into rounds ⅓ inch (1 cm) thick. Place them in a bowl, top with cold water, and agitate to loosen any dirt. Let sit for 5 minutes.

Meanwhile, in a medium saucepan, warm the oil over medium heat.

Scoop out the leeks, being careful to not disturb any sediment at the bottom of the bowl, and add them directly to the saucepan. Do not dry the leeks. Add the garlic and a generous pinch of flaky sea salt and cook, stirring often, until the leeks have softened, about 5 minutes.

Meanwhile, cut the asparagus into 1-inch (2.5 cm) lengths, leaving the tips intact.

Add the asparagus and a splash of the wine to the pan, cover, and cook for 3 minutes. Add the peas and cook until warmed through, 1 to 2 minutes.

Remove from the heat. Stir in the lemon zest and half of the lemon juice and season with salt and pepper to taste.

Tear the burrata and arrange on a serving platter. Top the burrata with the remaining lemon juice and season with salt.

Add the herbs to the saucepan, stir to combine, then pile the vegetables over the burrata. Finish with a generous drizzle of olive oil and a sprinkle of flaky sea salt.

JALAPEÑO POPPER TWICE-BAKED SWEET POTATOES

SERVES 4
PREP TIME: 25 MINUTES
COOK TIME: 1 HOUR 20 MINUTES
INACTIVE TIME: 30 MINUTES

FOR THE BAKED SWEET POTATOES

2 sweet potatoes, scrubbed clean and dried

Neutral oil

FOR THE BREAD CRUMB TOPPING

½ cup (66 g) no-salt-added plain bread crumbs

1 tablespoon extra-virgin olive oil

¼ teaspoon kosher salt

Smoked paprika

Freshly ground black pepper

FOR THE RANCH DRESSING

½ cup (120 ml) nondairy sour cream

2 tablespoons vegan mayonnaise

1 tablespoon unsweetened nondairy creamer

1 teaspoon fresh lemon juice

1 tablespoon chopped fresh dill

1 clove garlic, minced

1 tablespoon finely chopped fresh flat-leaf parsley

Kosher salt and freshly ground black pepper

Ingredients continue

If you're someone, like Priyanka, who wishes they could eat jalapeño poppers as their entire meal, then you're on the right page. Spicy, savory, cheesy, crunchy—everything you could ever want in a finger food—now as an entrée. The chef and author of *The Modern Tiffin* bakes whole sweet potatoes, halves them, scoops them out, mixes the filling with scallions, jalapeño, garlic, cheddar, cumin, and nondairy creamer and sour cream, puts the mixture back into the sweet potato shells, tops with bread crumbs and butter, bakes them again until golden and crispy, and serves them with ranch. So, rather than a bite of nostalgia, you can have an entire plate of it.

Bake the sweet potatoes: Preheat the oven to 375°F (190°C). Line a baking sheet with parchment paper.

Rub the sweet potatoes with some neutral oil to coat and place them onto the prepared baking sheet.

Bake until fork-tender, about 1 hour, flipping them over halfway through. Let rest until cool enough to handle, about 30 minutes. Leave the oven on.

Meanwhile, make the bread crumb topping: In a small bowl, toss the bread crumbs, oil, salt and a pinch each of smoked paprika and pepper until well combined.

Make the ranch dressing: In a medium bowl, whisk the sour cream, mayonnaise, creamer, lemon juice, dill, garlic, and parsley to combine. Season with salt and pepper to taste.

Make the filling: Halve the sweet potatoes lengthwise and carefully scoop out the flesh, keeping the shell intact. Transfer the flesh to a large bowl. Using a potato masher, mash the sweet potatoes until smooth.

Recipe continues

FOR THE FILLING

¼ cup (60 ml) unsweetened nondairy creamer

¼ cup (60 ml) nondairy sour cream

1 small jalapeño, deribbed, seeded, and diced

2 scallions, sliced

2 cloves garlic, minced

½ teaspoon ground cumin

¼ cup (30 g) vegan sharp cheddar shreds

Kosher salt and freshly ground black pepper

4 tablespoons (55 g) nondairy butter

Chopped fresh flat-leaf parsley, for garnish

Add the creamer, sour cream, jalapeño, scallions, garlic, cumin, and cheddar and mix to combine. Season with salt and pepper to taste.

Fill the sweet potato shells evenly with the filling. Divide the bread crumb topping evenly over the sweet potatoes. Place 1 tablespoon of the butter onto the center of each potato.

Bake until warmed through, about 15 minutes. Turn the oven to broil and bake until golden brown on top, 3 to 5 minutes.

Serve immediately with a sprinkling of chopped parsley and a drizzle of the ranch dressing.

Alon Shaya's
CHARRED CABBAGE WITH GARLICKY TAHINI

SERVES 4
PREP TIME: 25 MINUTES
COOK TIME: 1 HOUR 10 MINUTES
INACTIVE TIME: 30 MINUTES

FOR THE CABBAGE

½ cup (120 ml) extra-virgin olive oil

2 tablespoons kosher salt

2 cloves garlic, peeled

½ cup (120 ml) orange juice

½ cup (120 ml) rice vinegar, preferably seasoned

2 tablespoons sugar

1 jalapeño, deribbed, seeded, and sliced

1 whole star anise

Grated zest and juice of 1 lemon

1 medium head green cabbage

FOR THE GARLICKY TAHINI

¼ cup (60 ml) fresh lemon juice

2 cloves garlic, crushed

1¼ cups (300 ml) ice water, plus more as needed

3 tablespoons extra-virgin olive oil

1½ cups (360 ml) tahini

1 teaspoon kosher salt

TO FINISH

3 tablespoons extra-virgin olive oil

1 teaspoon kosher salt

¼ cup (35 g) pine nuts, toasted, for garnish

Large handful of fresh dill fronds, chopped, for garnish

Cabbage is a wildly underrated vegetable. We often see it prepared aggressively in sides like coleslaw, kimchi, and sauerkraut, but it is hardly ever treated simply, allowed to stand on its own. Alon is "crazy about its mellow sweetness," so he cooks it gently, in a deeply aromatic broth, until tender, then chars its edges to crisp, smoky perfection. The chef and cofounder of Pomegranate Hospitality finishes it with a drizzle of garlicky, lemony tahini and a handful of fresh dill to brighten it up like the star of the plate it was always meant to be.

Prepare the cabbage: In a deep pot that isn't too wide (ideally just large enough to hold a head of cabbage snugly), combine the olive oil, salt, garlic, orange juice, vinegar, sugar, jalapeño, star anise, lemon zest, lemon juice, and 2 quarts (1.9 L) water. Bring to a boil, then reduce the heat to medium and simmer for 10 minutes.

Meanwhile, trim any tough outer leaves from the cabbage and halve it through the core.

Carefully lower the cabbage halves into the pot, reduce the heat to low, and cook until the cabbage is easily pierced with a fork, but still resists slightly, 30 minutes to 1 hour 30 minutes, depending on the size.

Meanwhile, make the garlicky tahini: In a small bowl, combine the lemon juice and garlic and let steep for 30 minutes. Using a slotted spoon remove the garlic and discard. Adjust the consistency with a little ice water, as needed.

In a stand mixer fitted with the whisk, whip the tahini on high speed until glossy and light, about 10 minutes. Reduce the speed to medium and add the lemon juice and salt and continue mixing until the tahini has a uniformly tacky, almost fudgy consistency; it will seize at first, but then come together.

Recipe continues

Add the ice water about ¼ cup (60 ml) at a time, whipping well after each addition, until it forms a smooth, thick, and mousse-like texture. Set aside.

Using a large slotted spoon, carefully transfer the cabbage to a sheet pan to cool slightly. Discard the cooking liquid.

Meanwhile, position a rack in the upper third of the oven and preheat the broiler.

To finish: Leaving the stem ends intact, cut the cabbage halves through the core to make 4 quarters. Drain away any excess liquid, then remove any leaves that are so soft that they are falling off. Place each wedge on the sheet pan, curved side down. Brush the olive oil over the tops and season with the salt.

Broil, rotating the baking sheet front to back halfway through, until charred all along the edges, 7 to 9 minutes.

To serve, place the wedges on serving plates. Drizzle them with the garlicky tahini and garnish with the pine nuts and dill. Serve immediately.

Sheinelle's
TOASTED COCONUT PINEAPPLE BREAD PUDDING

SERVES 8
PREP TIME: 10 MINUTES
COOK TIME: 20 MINUTES

1 stick (4 ounces/115 g) unsalted butter, melted

1 cup (220 g) packed light brown sugar

¼ teaspoon kosher salt

3 large eggs

1 (20-ounce/567 g) can crushed pineapple, drained

1 (15-ounce/425 g) loaf challah bread, cut into 1-inch (2.5 cm) cubes

½ cup (26 g) toasted coconut flakes, for topping

When Sheinelle was growing up, her family spent a lot of time at church. After services, they would go to the church basement for some kind of food-filled event—and there was always pineapple stuffing. Made with just crushed pineapple, sugar, butter, eggs, and white bread, it was so simple but was a treat she looked forward to nonetheless. Here, we've zhuzhed it up a bit, using challah instead of white bread and topping it with toasted coconut, intended to be served as a side with ham, turkey, or chicken, though it could also be served as dessert with a scoop of ice cream or a dollop of whipped cream. Thankfully, it still captures the essence of the dish Sheinelle so frequently ate as a kid. "I am immediately transported from Studio 1A back to Wichita, Kansas," she says.

Preheat the oven to 350°F (180°C). Mist a 9 by 13-inch (22 by 33 cm) glass baking dish with cooking spray.

In a stand mixer fitted with the whisk, whip the butter, brown sugar, and salt to combine, about 2 minutes. Add the eggs, one at a time, allowing each to incorporate before adding the next. Continue whipping until light and fluffy, about 3 minutes.

Fold in the pineapple. Add the challah and fold until the bread is evenly coated. Transfer to the prepared baking dish and sprinkle the coconut flakes evenly over the top.

Bake until golden brown, 20 to 25 minutes.

Judy Joo's
KIMCHI FRIED RICE

SERVES 4
PREP TIME: 30 MINUTES
COOK TIME: 15 MINUTES
INACTIVE TIME: 30 MINUTES

FOR THE PORK

8 ounces (225 g) skinless pork belly, trimmed and cut into ½-inch (13 mm) pieces

2 tablespoons soy sauce

1 tablespoon toasted sesame oil

1 teaspoon grated garlic, grated on a Microplane

1 teaspoon grated fresh ginger, grated on a Microplane

1 tablespoon vegetable oil

Salt and freshly ground black pepper

FOR THE FRIED RICE

2 tablespoons soy sauce

1 tablespoon ssamjang (Korean dipping sauce)

2 teaspoons sugar

1 tablespoon toasted sesame oil

2 tablespoons vegetable oil

2 scallions, finely chopped

1 medium white onion, finely chopped

1¼ cups (355 g) kimchi with juices, cut into ¾-inch (2 cm) pieces

5 cups (700 g) cooked short-grain white rice, dried out on a tray

¼ cup (60 ml) Japanese mayonnaise, such as Kewpie

Salt and freshly ground black pepper

FOR SERVING (OPTIONAL)

Fried eggs, shredded roasted seaweed, toasted sesame seeds, and thinly sliced scallions

Known as kimchi bokkeumbap in Korean, this funky fried rice is a simple dish TV chef Judy's mom used to make for her as an after-school snack. And now, no matter the time of day, whether for breakfast, lunch, or dinner, it's her go-to comfort meal. This is a purist version, with just kimchi and pork, but you can throw anything into it—chopped-up lunch meats, frozen peas, broccoli, carrots—whatever needs to be used up in your fridge. Judy prefers extra-ripe kimchi for optimal fermented tang, and though not traditional, per se, the mayo adds a delectable creaminess.

Make the pork: In a large bowl, toss the pork belly, soy sauce, sesame oil, garlic, and ginger until well combined. Marinate for 30 minutes.

In a medium nonstick skillet, warm the vegetable oil over medium heat. Add the pork and the marinade and sauté until cooked through, about 4 minutes. Transfer the pork and any juices to a bowl. Season with salt and pepper to taste. Set aside.

Make the fried rice: In a small bowl, whisk together the soy, ssamjang, sugar, and sesame oil until the sugar is completely dissolved. Set aside.

In a large nonstick skillet, warm the vegetable oil over medium-high heat. Add the scallions and white onion and sauté, stirring often, until softened, about 2 minutes. Add the kimchi and cook, stirring often until softened, about 2 minutes. Add the rice and cook, using the back of a wooden spoon to break it up. Add the mayonnaise and the soy sauce mixture and cook for 3 to 4 minutes, stirring to ensure all ingredients are evenly combined.

Add the pork and any accumulated juices and mix well. Season with salt and pepper to taste.

To serve: Plate the rice into individual serving bowls. If desired, top each with a fried egg and a sprinkling of shredded roasted seaweed, sesame seeds, and scallions. Serve immediately.

Molly Yeh's
CRISPY BRUSSELS SPROUT CASSEROLE

SERVES 8
PREP TIME: 15 MINUTES
COOK TIME: 50 MINUTES

FOR THE TOPPING

1 cup (80 g) panko bread crumbs

½ cup (50 g) finely grated Parmesan cheese

1 tablespoon extra-virgin olive oil

½ teaspoon kosher salt

¼ teaspoon freshly ground black pepper

FOR THE BRUSSELS SPROUTS

Extra-virgin olive oil

8 ounces (225 g) diced pancetta

2 pounds (910 g) Brussels sprouts, quartered through the root end (or halved if small)

4 tablespoons (55 g) unsalted butter

1 large yellow onion, diced

Kosher salt and freshly ground black pepper

3 cloves garlic, sliced

2 teaspoons chopped fresh thyme

¼ teaspoon red pepper flakes, or to taste

3 tablespoons all-purpose flour

2 cups (480 ml) low-sodium chicken stock

1 cup (240 ml) heavy cream

2 teaspoons Dijon mustard

¼ cup (25 g) grated Parmesan cheese

Grated zest of 1 lemon

Molly, host of *Girl Meets Farm*, started making this casserole instead of the classic green bean version on Thanksgiving because the holiday falls during Brussels sprout season—not green bean season! Of course, this dish is great anytime during the colder months; it's special enough to be a holiday side but easy enough for a weeknight dinner. Brussels sprouts often get a bad rap because they can too easily devolve into skunky mushiness, but with a little help from their friends—lots of lemon and garlic, Dijon mustard, Parmesan, salty meat, and a crispy panko topping—they find their true form as the tastiest little cabbages ever.

Preheat the oven to 400°F (200°C).

Make the topping: In a medium bowl, toss together the panko, Parmesan, oil, salt, and pepper until well combined. Set aside.

Make the Brussels sprouts: In a large braiser or ovenproof skillet, warm a drizzle of olive oil over medium-high heat. Add the pancetta and cook, stirring periodically, until crispy, 8 to 10 minutes. Using a slotted spoon, transfer the pancetta to a plate.

Add 2 tablespoons olive oil and the Brussels sprouts to the pan and cook, tossing occasionally, until they begin to brown on the edges, 4 to 5 minutes.

Reduce the heat to medium, add the butter, and stir to melt. Add the onion, season with salt and pepper, and cook, stirring occasionally, until wilted, 4 to 5 minutes.

Add the garlic, thyme, and pepper flakes and cook until fragrant, about 1 minute. Sprinkle the flour over the vegetables and toss to coat. Gradually add the stock, stirring to incorporate. Add the cream, bring to a simmer,

Recipe continues

and cook until the sprouts are tender, 2 to 4 minutes. Stir in the mustard, Parmesan, lemon zest, and pancetta. Season with salt and black pepper to taste.

Transfer to a 9 by 13-inch (22 by 33 cm) baking dish and spread it evenly over the bottom. Sprinkle the topping evenly over the top.

Bake until bubbling and the bread crumbs are golden brown, about 20 minutes.

Daniel Boulud's
TARTIFLETTE (AKA CREAMY, CHEESY POTATOES)

SERVES 4
PREP TIME: 15 MINUTES
COOK TIME: 1 HOUR

3 medium Yukon Gold potatoes (about 14 ounces/400 g total), peeled

1 cup (240 ml) heavy cream

½ cup (120 ml) cup whole milk

Kosher salt and freshly ground black pepper

3 ounces (85 g) slab bacon, cut into matchsticks

1 clove garlic, finely chopped

1 small leek, white part only, thinly sliced and washed

5 ounces (140 g) Taleggio cheese, cut into ¼-inch (6 mm) slices

SWAP OPTION

Other cheeses you can try are Le Délice du Jura, fromage de Savoie, Robiola, Préféré de nos Montagnes, or a good Brie.

The tartiflette—a creamy baked casserole of potatoes, cream, bacon, and alliums—is the definition of French mountain food. After braving the elements, whether out skiing or shoveling the snow, there is no better dish, bubbling in the pan, to be greeted with. Chef and restaurateur Boulud's take on the comforting dish uses leeks instead of onions for a slightly sweeter taste, and Taleggio cheese instead of Reblochon because, frankly, it's a lot easier to find in the States.

Preheat the oven to 375°F (190°C).

Halve the potatoes lengthwise, and then in half again. Slice the quarters into ½-inch (13 mm) slices.

In a medium saucepan, combine the potatoes, cream, milk, ½ teaspoon salt, and a generous amount of pepper. Bring to a simmer and cook until the potatoes are very tender, about 20 minutes. Drain the potatoes into a colander set over a bowl to catch the cooking liquid. Set the potatoes and their cooking liquid aside.

Meanwhile, in a medium sauté pan, cook the bacon over medium-low heat until the fat has rendered and the bacon is crispy, 8 to 12 minutes. Using a slotted spoon, transfer the bacon to a small bowl, leaving the rendered fat behind.

To the sauté pan with the bacon fat, add the garlic and leek and cook over medium heat, stirring occasionally, until soft and tender, 5 to 7 minutes. Using a slotted spoon, transfer to the bowl with the bacon and stir to combine.

In an 8-inch (20 cm) round baking dish, scatter one-third of the bacon/leek mixture evenly over the bottom of the dish. Carefully spoon half of the potatoes evenly into the dish, gently pressing them down to create

Recipe continues

an even layer. Scatter another one-third of the bacon/leek mixture evenly over the potatoes. Scatter half the Taleggio over the top. Spoon the remaining potatoes over the cheese to create another layer. Sprinkle the remaining bacon/leek mixture evenly over the top.

Carefully and slowly, pour the potato cooking liquid evenly over the surface. Scatter the remaining cheese over the top.

Bake until the cream is bubbling and the cheese is golden, 20 to 25 minutes.

Finish with a sprinkling of pepper before serving.

Hoda's
BURNT BROCCOLI CHIPS

SERVES 2
PREP TIME: 15 MINUTES
COOK TIME: 35 MINUTES

FOR THE BROCCOLI

Kosher salt

1 head broccoli, cut into florets, leaving ½ inch (13 mm) of the stems

2 tablespoons olive oil, plus more for greasing

Freshly ground black pepper

FOR THE DIPPING SAUCE

½ cup (120 ml) Japanese mayonnaise, such as Kewpie

1 tablespoon honey

2 teaspoons soy sauce

1½ teaspoons fresh lemon juice

Lemon wedges, for serving

More than anything—sweet or savory—Hoda craves crunchy. And she always aims to eat a serving of vegetables every night. That's how this satisfying snack came to be. She blanches her broccoli, smashes it, seasons it, and bakes it till it's burnt. "I'll eat a big bowl of it like it's potato chips," she says, sometimes with this Japanese-inspired dipping sauce. Other times, she'll serve it as a side with her Two-Ingredient Ponzu Cod (page 146) for dinner.

Make the broccoli: Preheat the oven to 400°F (200°C).

Fill a large bowl with ice and water and line a baking sheet with paper towels. Bring a large pot of lightly salted water to a boil. Add the broccoli and cook until tender but not too soft, 6 to 8 minutes. Using a spider, immediately transfer the broccoli to the prepared ice bath. Once cooled, transfer the broccoli to the paper towels and with additional paper towels, gently press down to remove as much moisture as possible.

Drizzle the oil across a large sheet pan. Add the broccoli, spacing the floret 2 inches (5 cm) apart. Lightly grease the bottom of a large mason jar or dry measuring cup and firmly press the broccoli to smash into a chip ⅛ inch (3 mm) thick. Season with salt and pepper.

Place the sheet pan in the hottest part of the oven and bake until the broccoli is well charred, about 25 minutes, flipping when the bottoms are browned.

Meanwhile, make the dipping sauce: In a medium bowl, whisk the mayonnaise, honey, soy sauce, and lemon juice until well combined. Transfer to a dip bowl.

Transfer the broccoli to a serving plate and serve immediately with lemon wedges and the dipping sauce.

 TIP

Press more firmly on the stem side to evenly flatten the broccoli floret.

Al's
SWEET POTATO POON WITH TOASTY MARSHMALLOWS

SERVES 12
PREP TIME: 15 MINUTES
COOK TIME: 1 HOUR 10 MINUTES

Softened butter, for the baking dish

Kosher salt

6 large sweet potatoes (about 4 pounds/1.8 kg total), peeled and cut into 2-inch (5 cm) cubes

1 stick (4 ounces/115 g) unsalted butter

1 cup (120 g) all-purpose flour

1 cup (220 g) firmly packed dark brown sugar

2 tablespoons baking powder

1 teaspoon ground cinnamon

1 teaspoon freshly grated nutmeg

1 teaspoon ground allspice

1 cup (245 g) drained canned crushed pineapple

1 (16-ounce/455 g) container marshmallow crème

2 cups (92 g) mini marshmallows

You didn't think we'd write a whole cookbook without including Al's mom's famous sweet potato poon, did you? Well, here she is, in all her glory. He's not sure where his mom came up with the recipe—nor its infamous name—but it became a Thanksgiving staple in the Roker household regardless. This marshmallow-topped casserole never failed to give them a good laugh, he says, "as my mom always got distracted as soon as it went under the broiler, which caused the smoke alarm to go off." In this updated recipe, marshmallow crème is piped on top to maximize the surface area for toastiness—just don't forget to keep an eye on it!

Preheat the oven to 350°F (180°C). Butter a 9 by 13-inch (22 by 33 cm) baking dish.

In a large soup pot, bring generously salted water to a rolling boil. Add the sweet potatoes, return to a boil, and cook until soft, about 12 minutes. Drain the potatoes and transfer them to a large bowl.

Add the butter to the sweet potatoes and use a potato masher to mash the potatoes until they're as smooth as possible. Add the flour, brown sugar, baking powder, cinnamon, nutmeg, allspice, ½ teaspoon salt, and the pineapple and mix until well combined.

Transfer the mixture to the prepared baking dish and spread it evenly across the bottom.

Bake until browned, about 45 minutes. Remove from the oven.

Increase the oven temperature to broil.

Meanwhile, transfer the marshmallow crème to a large piping bag fitted with a large round tip. Pipe the marshmallow evenly over the top, then sprinkle the mini marshmallows evenly over the crème. Broil until the marshmallows are nicely toasted, about 1 minute.

Home Base:
PASTA & NOODLES

Yes, pasta gets its own section because, well, it's pasta. It's where we so often return when seeking comfort, because it feels like home. Most of these dishes are on the lighter side (the zucchini pasta and seafood linguine will make you feel like you're basking in the Italian sun), but they are all satisfying enough to be served on their own (especially the beef and broccoli lo mein). When in doubt about what to make for dinner, use your noodle—you won't regret it.

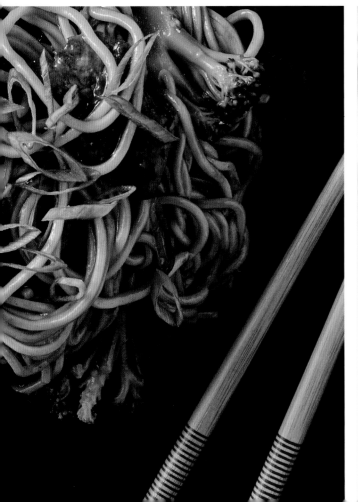

Gaby Dalkin's

ZESTY ZUCCHINI PASTA

SERVES 4
PREP TIME: 15 MINUTES
COOK TIME: 40 MINUTES

¼ cup (60 ml) extra-virgin olive oil, plus more for serving

4 smal -l green zucchini (about 1½ pounds/680 g), sliced into ⅛-inch (3 mm) rounds

3 small leeks, white parts only, sliced into ⅛-inch (3 mm) rounds

2 cloves garlic, minced

Sea salt

1 pound (455 g) spaghetti

2½ cups (10 ounces/280 g) finely grated pecorino or Parmesan, or a combo

Grated zest of 1 lemon

1 teaspoon freshly ground black pepper, plus for serving

2 tablespoons unsalted butter

2 large handfuls fresh basil, torn

We all wish we could hop on a plane to Italy for dinner, but when that's not possible (nearly 100 percent of the time), Gaby makes this dish, one that originated in the town of Nerano on the Amalfi Coast in southern Italy. Its star ingredient is super-tender zucchini that melts in your mouth, paired with pasta, plenty of cheese, and pepper. The author and founder of What's Gaby Cooking adds leeks for their subtle sweetness and lemon zest for a bit of brightness. "It screams summer on the ocean," she says. "All you need is a glass of crisp white wine and you're in business."

In a large sauté pan, heat the olive oil over medium heat. Add the zucchini and leeks and cook, stirring often, until softened, about 25 minutes.

Add the garlic and cook until fragrant, about 1 minute. Remove from the heat, season with salt and pepper to taste, and set the skillet aside.

In a large soup pot, bring generously salted water to a rolling boil.

Add the spaghetti and cook to al dente according to the package directions. Reserving 1 cup (240 ml) of the pasta water, drain the pasta.

Meanwhile, in a medium bowl, stir together the pecorino, lemon zest, and black pepper to combine. Set aside ¾ cup (80 g) of the mixture for serving.

Return the skillet to medium-high heat. Add the spaghetti, butter, and cheese mixture and cook, stirring constantly, adding the reserved pasta water as needed, until a creamy sauce forms.

Transfer to a large platter and top with the reserved cheese mixture and torn basil. Drizzle a bit of olive oil over the top as well as a few grinds of black pepper and serve.

Jet Tila's
BEEF & BROCCOLI LO MEIN

SERVES 4
PREP TIME: 10 MINUTES
COOK TIME: 10 MINUTES
INACTIVE TIME: 10 MINUTES

FOR THE MARINATED BEEF

1 pound (455 g) flank steak

1 tablespoon soy sauce

1 teaspoon toasted sesame oil

1 teaspoon baking soda

1 teaspoon cornstarch

FOR THE SAUCE

6 tablespoons (90 ml) oyster sauce

2 teaspoons toasted sesame oil

2 tablespoons soy sauce

½ cup (120 ml) chicken stock

1 tablespoon sugar

2 teaspoons cornstarch

FOR THE LO MEIN

1 (12-ounce/340 g) bag steam-in-bag broccoli florets

3 tablespoons canola oil

2 teaspoons minced garlic

1 tablespoon thinly sliced fresh ginger

8 ounces (225 g) fresh lo mein noodles

3 scallions, sliced on the bias

When ordering Chinese takeout, Jet always finds himself eating beef and broccoli with a side of lo mein. Inevitably, the two dishes find themselves intermingled on his plate, creating the ultimate American Chinese mashup meal. So, the host of *Ready Jet Cook* finally decided to intentionally merge the dishes, cooking the beef, broccoli, and noodles together and binding them with oyster sauce, never to be served in separate cartons again.

Marinate the beef: Slice the beef with the grain into sections 2 inches (5 cm) wide. Cut each section, against the grain, into thin strips and place them into a large bowl. Add the soy sauce, sesame oil, baking soda, and cornstarch and toss to combine. Let sit for at least 10 minutes at room temperature, or up to overnight in the refrigerator.

Meanwhile, make the sauce: In a small bowl, whisk together the oyster sauce, sesame oil, soy sauce, chicken stock, sugar, and cornstarch to combine. Set aside.

Prepare the lo mein: Place the steam-in-bag broccoli into the microwave and cook, until barely fork-tender, about 5 minutes. Transfer to a plate to air-dry for 5 minutes.

Meanwhile, in a large skillet or wok, warm the oil over high heat until you see wisps of white smoke. Add the garlic and ginger and cook until lightly browned and fragrant, about 20 seconds. Add the beef and sauté, stirring often, until cooked to medium and browned, 1 to 2 minutes.

Add the noodles and broccoli and cook, tossing often, until the broccoli begins to soften and turn bright green, 1 to 2 minutes. Add the sauce and cook, stirring to combine until thickened and all ingredients are evenly coated and the beef is cooked through, 1 to 2 minutes.

Plate the lo mein, garnish with scallions, and serve immediately.

 TIP

It's important to get all your ingredients ready. Once you start stir-frying, the dish will come together in minutes!

SWAP OPTION

If you can't find lo mein noodles, cook 8 ounces (225 g) fettuccine or linguine until al dente, rinse until no longer sticky, and toss into the pan.

Eric Ripert's
LINGUINE WITH CLAMS & MUSSELS

SERVES 4
PREP TIME: 10 MINUTES
COOK TIME: 25 MINUTES
INACTIVE TIME: 1 HOUR

16 Manila clams

16 mussels

Kosher salt

1 pound (455 g) linguine

1 cup (240 ml) dry white wine

2 tablespoons extra-virgin olive oil

2 cloves garlic, finely chopped

½ teaspoon red pepper flakes

1 tablespoon finely chopped fresh parsley

Juice of ½ lemon

2 tablespoons unsalted butter, at room temperature

"Each time I eat this dish, which comes from Naples, it transports me right to summer in Italy watching the fishing boats," says Eric, chef and co-owner of Le Bernardin. In the classic recipe—linguine alle vongole—only clams are used, but he likes to add mussels, too, for a little sweetness and color. And though this bright and briny dish might evoke luxurious Mediterranean memories, it's simple to pull off at home.

Scrub the clams and mussels under cold running water, removing any broken or open shells, and place in a large bowl. Fill with room-temperature water and 2 tablespoons kosher salt and mix to combine. Let sit for 1 hour.

Remove the shellfish, without disturbing the bottom of the bowl, rinse under cold water and transfer to a bowl.

Bring a large pot of lightly salted water to a boil. Add the pasta and cook to al dente, about 10 minutes. Drain.

Meanwhile, in a large sauté pan, warm the oil over medium heat. Add the garlic and cook until softened, 1 to 2 minutes. Add the clams, mussels, and white wine, cover with a tight-fitting lid, and shake gently to evenly disperse the shellfish. Increase the heat to medium-high and steam, using tongs to transfer them to a bowl as they open, until all the mussels and clams have opened, 5 to 7 minutes. Discard any that do not open.

Add the linguine, pepper flakes, parsley, lemon juice, and butter to the sauté pan and toss, coating the pasta with the sauce until the butter is melted. Return the shellfish to the pan, toss to combine, and season with salt to taste, if necessary.

Divide into warm bowls and serve immediately.

 TIP

When preparing, take care to smell, wash, and rinse the clams and mussels, and when plating, try to serve the same number of shellfish on each plate and reserve some broth to sprinkle on at the end.

Adam Richman's
EASY AS SPAGHETTI PIE

SERVES 6
PREP TIME: 20 MINUTES
COOK TIME: 35 MINUTES
INACTIVE TIME: 45 MINUTES

2 tablespoons extra-virgin olive oil, plus more for greasing

2 cloves garlic, chopped

2 medium zucchini, cut into ¼-inch (6 mm) dice

Kosher salt

1 cup (245 g) whole-milk ricotta cheese

1½ cups (160 g) finely grated Parmesan cheese

1½ teaspoons onion powder

3 large eggs

1 cup (240 ml) tomato paste

1½ cups (170 g) shredded mozzarella cheese

8 ounces (225 g) spaghetti, cooked to al dente, at room temperature

½ cup (12 g) chiffonade-cut basil

Leftover spaghetti is a late-night delicacy. There is nothing like stealing a bite directly from the container in the fridge, especially after a few too many drinks. But if you're willing to put in a little more effort, you can turn it into a masterpiece: spaghetti pie. TV host and cookbook author Adam's recipe went viral on the show ten years ago, so in honor of its viral-versary, he has a fresh, meatless take on the dish. It operates on the same principle as baked ziti, so feel free to use whatever ingredients you have on hand.

Preheat the oven to 350°F (180°C). Grease a 9-inch (22 cm) pie dish with some olive oil.

In a large skillet, warm the 2 tablespoons olive oil over medium-high heat. Add the garlic and sauté, stirring constantly, until the garlic just begins to take on some color, about 20 seconds. Add the zucchini and a generous pinch of salt and cook, stirring occasionally, until fork-tender, 4 to 5 minutes. Transfer to a bowl and refrigerate to cool down for 15 minutes.

Meanwhile, in a medium bowl, stir together the ricotta, ½ cup (60 g) of the Parmesan, and the onion powder until well combined. Refrigerate.

In a large bowl, whisk together the eggs and ¾ cup (195 g) of the tomato paste until smooth. Stir in 1 cup (110 g) of the mozzarella and the remaining 1 cup (100 g) Parmesan to combine. Add the spaghetti and zucchini mixture and toss to combine.

Spread the remaining ¼ cup (65 g) tomato paste, as best as possible, onto the bottom of the prepared pie dish. Add the spaghetti mixture and press it evenly into the dish. Sprinkle the remaining ½ cup (60 g) mozzarella evenly over the top.

Bake until the cheese is melted and the pie is crispy around the edges, 30 to 35 minutes.

Meanwhile, remove the ricotta mixture from the refrigerator.

Let the spaghetti pie cool for 30 minutes.

Spread the ricotta mixture evenly over the pie and sprinkle the basil evenly over the top. Cut into wedges and serve.

Dylan's
ANY-GREENS-PESTO PASTA

SERVES 6
PREP TIME: 10 MINUTES
COOK TIME: 25 MINUTES

Kosher salt

1 pound (454 g) gemelli pasta

2 tablespoons plus ½ cup (150 ml) extra-virgin olive oil

2 cloves garlic, smashed and peeled

⅓ cup (50 g) cubed Parmigiano-Reggiano cheese, plus grated for serving

¼ cup (25 g) walnuts, toasted

1 (10-ounce/283 g) container baby spinach

Freshly ground black pepper

"This recipe was created out of necessity," says Dylan. **Like many of us, she rarely has all the fresh ingredients for a traditional pesto, but she always has garlic, cheese, some type of nut, and a bunch of greens that are begging to be used before wilting. Throw all those ingredients into the blender with some olive oil and you've got yourself a vibrantly verdant—and sneakily nutritious—sauce to perk up your pasta. "This was literally an experiment, and my kids were obsessed, and now it's on weekly rotation,"** she says. **"The hardest part is waiting for the pasta to cook!"**

In a large soup pot, bring generously salted water to a rolling boil. Add the pasta and cook to al dente according to the package directions. Reserving 1 cup (240 ml) of the pasta water, drain the pasta.

Meanwhile, in a small skillet, heat 2 tablespoons of the oil over medium-high heat. Add the garlic and sauté until lightly toasted, about 2 minutes. Remove and set aside to cool for 5 minutes.

In a blender or food processor, pulse the Parmigiano until finely grated. Add the cooled garlic/oil mixture, walnuts, half of the spinach, and the remaining ½ cup (120 ml) olive oil and pulse until smooth. Using a silicone spatula, scrape down the sides of the blender, add the remaining spinach, and pulse until smooth. Add the pasta water, a splash at a time, until a creamy sauce is created. (You may not use all of it.) Season with salt and pepper to taste.

In a large bowl, toss the pasta with as much pesto as you'd like, mixing until the pasta is evenly coated. Serve immediately with a sprinkling of grated Parmigiano.

 TIP

This recipe makes about 1 cup of leftover sauce, so you can freeze it and thaw it when you're in need of an even speedier dinner.

MIDNIGHT SPAGHETTI

SERVES 2
PREP TIME: 5 MINUTES
COOK TIME: 15 MINUTES

Kosher salt

8 ounces (225 g) spaghetti, preferably from Gragnano

⅓ cup (80 ml) extra-virgin olive oil, plus more for finishing

3 whole cloves garlic, peeled

2 anchovy fillets

Pinch of Italian chile flakes

Freshly grated Parmigiano-Reggiano cheese, for serving

This is the pasta Stefano makes late at night (or in the wee hours of the morning) after one too many spritzes or Negronis. Consisting only of pantry staples—spaghetti, olive oil, garlic, anchovies, and red pepper flakes—this recipe delivers a satisfying, booze-absorbing meal in mere moments. "I know it says it serves two, but there are times I can easily take down both servings myself," the chef-partner at New York City's Rezdôra admits. Don't forget a heavy dusting of Parmigiano-Reggiano at the end (no one will ask you to say "when").

In a large soup pot, bring generously salted water to a rolling boil.

Add the spaghetti and cook to 2 minutes shy of al dente according to the package directions. Reserving ½ cup (120 ml) of the pasta water, drain the pasta.

Meanwhile, in a medium saucepan, combine the oil, garlic, and anchovies and cook over low heat, stirring often, until the garlic is golden and the anchovies have melted into the oil, about 5 minutes. Remove the garlic and discard.

Add the chile flakes, reserved pasta water, and spaghetti and cook, stirring until the sauce comes together and the pasta is cooked through, about 2 minutes.

Serve immediately with a drizzle of oil and a very generous dusting of Parmigiano-Reggiano.

The Lead:
MAINS

And now, for our top story of the day—the main course. This is, of course, the meat of the book—shout-out to chicken, beef, and pork—but we've also got fish and vegetarian options, too. There are plenty of weeknight dinner ideas, like cast-iron paella and kung pao eggplant, as well as holiday-worthy centerpieces, like coffee-braised brisket and whole roast jerk chicken. In this section, Al makes good use of his cast-iron skillet with pork chops and rib-eye steak, while Dylan shares the meatballs and chicken piccata her kids constantly request.

Al's
CAST-IRON RIB-EYE WITH ANCHOVY BUTTER

SERVES 2
PREP TIME: 10 MINUTES
COOK TIME: 15 MINUTES
INACTIVE TIME: 25 MINUTES

FOR THE ANCHOVY COMPOUND BUTTER

½ medium shallot, roughly chopped

3 cloves garlic, peeled but whole

1 tablespoon fresh rosemary leaves

4 anchovy fillets

¼ teaspoon smoked paprika

1 teaspoon kosher salt

1 stick (4 ounces/115 g) unsalted butter, at room temperature

FOR THE RIB-EYE

1 bone-in rib-eye steak, 1½ inches (4 cm) thick

1 tablespoon vegetable oil

Kosher salt and freshly ground black pepper

 TIPS

Cut off a small chunk of the butter at a time, and use it to flavor any number of meats, sauces, or even pastas.

The compound butter can be made in advance and stored in the refrigerator for up to 1 week or in the freezer for up to 3 months.

According to Al, a great steak doesn't need much more than salt and pepper. But he does have a "secret weapon" that takes his rib-eye to the next level: anchovies. He will melt a few fillets in a pan with butter before he drops the steak in. This recipe takes that idea and turns it into an umami bomb you can keep in your fridge or freezer to throw into the pan at a moment's notice: anchovy compound butter. Soften it, slice it, melt it, and use it to infuse anything—steak, chicken, fish, or even vegetables—with bright and briny flavor.

And if you have anchovy naysayers in your midst, Al says, "Don't tell people they're in there—they'll just thank you for a delicious meal."

Make the anchovy compound butter: In a mini chopper, pulse the shallot, garlic, rosemary, anchovies, smoked paprika, and salt until finely chopped. Add the softened butter and pulse, scraping down the sides as needed, until evenly combined.

Transfer the mixture to a piece of parchment paper and roll into a cylinder. Wrap the cylinder tightly in plastic wrap and refrigerate.

Cook the rib-eye: Preheat the oven to 400°F (200°C). Let the steak sit at room temperature for 20 minutes.

In a large cast-iron skillet, warm the oil over medium-high heat. Generously season both sides of the steak with salt and pepper. Add the steak to the skillet and cook, undisturbed, until well seared, about 3 minutes. Flip the steak and cook for an additional 3 minutes.

Transferring the skillet to the oven and cook until the center reaches an internal temperature of 135°F (57°C), about 9 minutes. Transfer the steak to a cutting board and let rest for 5 to 7 minutes.

Meanwhile, place a generous pat of the anchovy butter into the skillet to melt.

Slice the steak, shingle on a plate, and top with the melted anchovy compound butter. Serve immediately.

Bobby Flay's
HONEY MUSTARD GRILLED CHICKEN THIGHS WITH HERBY OLIVE RELISH

SERVES 6
PREP TIME: 10 MINUTES
COOK TIME: 25 MINUTES

FOR THE RELISH

1 cup (125 g) Sicilian green olives, pitted and coarsely chopped

3 tablespoons thinly sliced scallions

3 tablespoons roughly chopped fresh mint

3 tablespoons roughly chopped fresh cilantro

2 tablespoons extra-virgin olive oil

½ cup (60 g) Sicilian pistachios, toasted and chopped

Grated zest and juice of 1 lime

Kosher salt and freshly ground black pepper

FOR THE GLAZED CHICKEN

½ cup (120 ml) Dijon mustard

¼ cup (60 ml) honey

Kosher salt and freshly ground black pepper

8 boneless, skinless chicken thighs

2 tablespoons extra-virgin olive oil

FOR SERVING

Butter lettuce leaves

Fresh mint sprigs

Fresh cilantro leaves

"Chicken thighs are secretly one of my favorite things to eat," says Bobby, chef at Brasserie B. This particular dish hits on so many things he craves: a sweet and assertive glaze made with honey and Dijon mustard; a punchy, crunchy relish made of olives, mint, and pistachios; and, of course, juicy chicken thighs, which are the perfect vehicle for the aforementioned condiments. "I could eat this all day long," he says.

Make the relish: In a medium bowl, mix together the olives, scallions, mint, cilantro, olive oil, pistachios, lime zest, lime juice, and salt and pepper to taste. Set aside.

Make the chicken: Preheat a grill pan over high heat.

Meanwhile, in a small bowl, whisk together the mustard and honey to combine and season with salt and pepper to taste. Set aside.

Brush the chicken with the olive oil and season with salt and pepper. Working in batches, cook the chicken smooth side down on the grill pan and cook until lightly charred, 4 to 5 minutes.

Using tongs, flip the chicken and brush the tops with the glaze. Cook until the thighs are cooked through and register 165°F (73°C) on an instant-read thermometer, 4 to 5 minutes.

Flip the chicken, glaze the other side, and cook for 1 minute. Transfer the chicken to a cutting board and let rest for 1 to 2 minutes.

To serve: Slice the chicken into strips, place it on a serving platter, and top with the relish. Serve hot with butter lettuce, and mint, and cilantro for wrapping.

Hoda's
TWO-INGREDIENT PONZU COD

SERVES 4
PREP TIME: 5 MINUTES
COOK TIME: 25 MINUTES

4 black cod fillets (6 ounces/ 170 g each)

1 (10-ounce/296 ml) bottle ponzu sauce

No, your eyes are not deceiving you: This recipe really has only two ingredients. To be honest with you, we debated about adding ingredients to it to beef it up a bit, but that's just not how Hoda cooks. "I'm all about simplicity," she says. "I want to make the best thing with the least amount of effort." This dish, an extremely pared-down take on Nobu's famous miso black cod, is the epitome of that attitude. You plop the fish in a baking dish, pour in ponzu—"glug, glug, glug" is how she measures it—and pop it in the oven. When you take it out, "It's like eating butter," she says.

Preheat the oven to 375°F (190°C).

Place the cod fillets into a 9 by 13-inch (22 by 33 cm) baking dish. Pour the ponzu sauce over the tops of the fillets. It should come halfway up the fish in the baking dish.

Bake until the cod is opaque, flakes easily with a fork, and an instant-read thermometer reads 145°F (62°C) when inserted into the thickest part, about 25 minutes.

 TIP

Hoda typically serves this dish with rice or couscous and some kind of veg—like her Broccoli Chips (page 123).

Dylan's
MELT-IN-YOUR-MOUTH MEATBALLS

MAKES ABOUT 16 MEATBALLS;
**   SERVES 8**
PREP TIME: 25 MINUTES
COOK TIME: 35 MINUTES

3 tablespoons extra-virgin olive oil

⅔ cup (100 g) Italian-style bread crumbs

1 cup (240 ml) whole milk

½ pound (225 g) ground beef (preferably 80/20)

½ pound (225 g) ground pork

½ pound (225 g) ground veal

1½ teaspoons kosher salt

½ teaspoon freshly ground black pepper

1½ teaspoons garlic powder

1½ teaspoons onion powder

1 small yellow onion (6 ounces/ 170 g), finely chopped

2 tablespoons finely chopped fresh parsley

¼ cup (25 g) finely grated Pecorino Romano cheese

2 large eggs, beaten

"I'm very picky when it comes to meatballs," Dylan says. "They should be so soft and pillowy, I don't need to use a knife." And that's exactly what makes these meatballs—passed down from her mother-in-law, Denise—so special. With a combination of beef, pork, and veal, plus plenty of eggs, they crisp up nicely, soak up sauce, and melt in your mouth—no knife required.

Preheat the oven to 375°F (190°C). Grease a large sheet pan with the olive oil, spreading it evenly on the bottom.

In a medium bowl, mix the bread crumbs and milk to combine. Let soak for 5 minutes.

Meanwhile, in a large bowl, gently toss the beef, pork, and veal to break the meat up. Sprinkle the meat with salt, pepper, garlic powder, and onion powder and gently toss to combine.

Add the onion, parsley, pecorino, and soaked bread crumb mixture to the meat and mix to combine. Add the eggs and mix until just combined.

Using a ¼-cup (60 ml) cookie scoop, portion the meat and gently roll each scoop into a ball, placing it onto the prepared sheet pan.

Bake until browned and the center of the meatballs register 160°F (70°C), about 35 minutes.

 TIP

Leftover meatballs can be stored, unsauced, in zip-top bags in the freezer for up to 2 months. Thaw in the refrigerator overnight, then warm in sauce before serving.

Jenna's
TEX-MEX ENCHILADAS

SERVES 4
PREP TIME: 10 MINUTES
COOK TIME: 35 MINUTES

1 tablespoon extra-virgin olive oil

1 pound (455 g) ground beef (80/20)

½ teaspoon kosher salt

1 (1-ounce/28 g) packet taco seasoning mix

1 cup (160 g) canned black beans, drained and rinsed

1 cup (140 g) frozen fire-roasted corn, thawed

2 (10-ounce/283 g) cans red enchilada sauce

3 cups (335 g) finely shredded Mexican cheese blend

8 (8-inch/20 cm) flour tortillas

Fresh cilantro leaves, for garnish

Lime wedges, for squeezing

It's a Bush tradition to eat enchiladas on Christmas Eve. "The first year my husband spent Christmas with my family, he was like, 'Wait, where's the ham?'" Jenna says. "He couldn't believe that that was the way we celebrated." But this Tex-Mex dish, which features flour tortillas rolled into tubes filled with beef, black beans, roasted corn, and cheese, immersed in red chile sauce and baked with more sauce and cheese, is a beautiful—and very Texan—way to celebrate the holiday.

Preheat the oven to 350°F (180°C).

In a large skillet, warm the oil over medium-high heat. Add the beef and salt and sauté, breaking the meat into small bits with a wooden spoon, until cooked through, about 5 minutes.

Add the taco seasoning, stir to combine, and cook until it's fully absorbed into the meat, about 1 minute. Remove from the heat. Add the beans and corn and stir to combine.

Spread half of the enchilada sauce evenly over the bottom of a 9 by 13-inch (22 by 33 cm) casserole dish.

Lay a tortilla on a clean work surface. Add a slightly heaping ½-cup (80 g) scoop of the meat filling across the center. Sprinkle ¼ cup (30 g) of the cheese over the filling. Roll the tortilla into a tight tube and place it, seam side down, into the casserole dish. Repeat with the remaining 7 tortillas.

Pour the remaining enchilada sauce evenly over the tops of the rolled tortillas. Sprinkle the remaining 1 cup (110 g) of cheese evenly over the top. Tent the casserole dish loosely with foil.

Bake for 20 minutes. Remove the foil and bake until the cheese is golden brown, about 10 minutes.

Garnish with cilantro leaves and serve with lime wedges for squeezing.

Elizabeth Heiskell's
KICKIN' FRIED CHICKEN

SERVES 4
PREP TIME: 10 MINUTES
COOK TIME: 30 MINUTES

3 quarts (2.8 L) vegetable oil

2 cups (240 g) all-purpose flour

3 tablespoons seasoned salt, such as Lawry's

2 tablespoons Cajun seasoning

2 tablespoons Greek seasoning, such as Al Roker's on page 198

1 whole chicken, broken down into 10 pieces

If Elizabeth has said it once on the show, she's said it a hundred times: "Honey, you need to get the oil as hot as the hinges of hell." That's how you get the crispiest fried chicken. To ensure it's at scorching status, flick a few droplets of water into the oil, and if it sizzles, it's ready to go. And, for goodness' sake, make sure your flour is properly seasoned. If you follow these very straightforward rules, you will be rewarded with the best fried chicken there is. So go ahead and enjoy it, because, as the author of *Come On Over!* says, "You are going to be dead a long time."

In a large Dutch oven, heat the oil over high heat to 375°F (190°C). Line a baking sheet with paper towels and have near the stove.

In a large bowl, whisk together the flour, seasoned salt, Cajun seasoning, and Greek seasoning until well combined.

Working in batches of 3 pieces, coat the chicken in the flour mixture and, using tongs, add to the hot oil, moving the meat around every now and then, until deep golden brown and an instant-read thermometer reads 165°F (75°C) when inserted into the thickest part of the chicken, 10 to 12 minutes. Transfer to the paper towels to drain before serving.

 TIP
Serve this with Camila Alves McConaughey's No-Mayo Coleslaw (page 77) to add a little freshness.

Al's
PAN-SEARED PORK CHOPS WITH ZIPPY GREEN SAUCE

SERVES 4
PREP TIME: 10 MINUTES
COOK TIME: 20 MINUTES
INACTIVE TIME: 5 MINUTES

FOR THE ZIPPY GREEN SAUCE

3 cloves garlic, peeled but whole

½ jalapeño

1½ cups (40 g) fresh cilantro leaves and tender stems

¼ teaspoon Aleppo pepper

½ teaspoon kosher salt

¼ teaspoon freshly ground black pepper

1 tablespoon fresh lime juice

½ cup (120 ml) extra-virgin olive oil

FOR THE PORK CHOPS

4 bone in pork chops (10 ounces/285 g each), 1 inch (2.5 cm) thick

Kosher salt

¼ cup (32 g) Al's Greek-Style Seasoning Blend (page 198)

1 tablespoon vegetable oil

When it comes to pork chops—or really any meat—Al likes to "keep it simple." He'll season it with his homemade Greek-style seasoning blend, give it a good sear in his cast-iron skillet, and call it a day. But when he's looking to spice things up, he whips up this sauce that can only be described as "zippy," thanks to garlic, jalapeño, cilantro, and lime. And while it pairs perfectly with pork, this sauce can be used to add a little zip to pretty much anything—chicken, fish, steak, you name it.

Make the zippy green sauce: In a mini chopper, mince the garlic and jalapeño. Add the cilantro leaves and pulse until finely chopped. Add the Aleppo pepper, salt, black pepper, lime juice, and olive oil and pulse to combine.

Cook the pork chops: Preheat the oven to 400°F (200°C).

Generously season both sides of each pork chop with salt. Season both sides of the pork chops with the spice blend, pressing it into the meat to adhere.

Meanwhile, in a large cast-iron skillet, warm the oil over medium-high heat. Add 2 of the pork chops and sear for 3 minutes. Flip and cook until golden brown on the second side. Use tongs to pick up the chops and sear the opposite end and sides for 4 to 5 minutes. Transfer to a quarter-sheet pan and tent with foil. Repeat with the remaining 2 chops.

Transfer to the oven and bake, uncovered, until an instant-read thermometer registers 140°F (60°C), about 4 minutes.

Tent with foil and let rest for 5 minutes before slicing and serving with the sauce.

Ayesha Nurdjaja's

Ayesha Nurdjaja's
CHICKEN SHAWARMA WITH WHITE SAUCE

SERVES 6
PREP TIME: 25 MINUTES
COOK TIME: 30 TO 40 MINUTES
INACTIVE TIME: 4 HOURS

FOR THE WHITE SAUCE

¼ cup (60 ml) crème fraîche

¼ cup (60 ml) mayonnaise

½ cup (120 ml) full-fat yogurt

1 small clove garlic, finely grated

1 teaspoon garlic powder

1 teaspoon onion powder

½ teaspoon kosher salt, plus more to taste

½ teaspoon freshly ground black pepper

¼ teaspoon red pepper flakes

1 teaspoon fresh lemon juice, plus more to taste

1 teaspoon sherry vinegar

Ingredients continue

MAKE AHEAD

The white sauce can be made up to 4 days in advance.

There is nothing like a warm pita stuffed to the brim with meat freshly shaved off the spit. But it would be impossible to make shawarma at home, right? Not so, says Ayesha, chef-partner at Shuka and Shukette in New York City. It's actually quite easy—no rotisserie required. By marinating thinly sliced chicken in garlic paste, olive oil, lemon juice, and a Middle Eastern spice blend, you can penetrate the meat with flavor and tenderize it until succulent. Roast it until crispy around the edges, slather it with tangy, garlicky white sauce (which you will want to put on everything from here on out), and you have yourself something straight out of your favorite food stall.

Make the white sauce: In a medium bowl, whisk together the crème fraîche, mayonnaise, yogurt, grated garlic, garlic powder, onion powder, salt, black pepper, pepper flakes, lemon juice, and sherry vinegar until well combined.

Transfer to an airtight container and refrigerate, allowing the flavors to meld for at least 4 hours. Add additional lemon juice and salt, to taste, if necessary.

Make the chicken shawarma: In a large bowl, whisk together the garlic paste, ½ cup (120 ml) of the oil, the salt, turmeric, cinnamon, black pepper, cumin, smoked paprika, and lemon juice until well combined.

Add the chicken and onion and toss, massaging the marinade into the chicken, until fully coated. Cover tightly with plastic wrap and refrigerate for a minimum of 4 hours, but preferably for 48 hours.

When ready to cook, preheat the oven to 425°F (220°C). Line two sheet pans with foil and, dividing evenly, drizzle with the remaining ¼ cup (60 ml) olive oil.

Recipe continues

FOR THE CHICKEN SHAWARMA

2 tablespoons garlic paste

¾ cup (180 ml) extra-virgin olive oil

2 teaspoons kosher salt

1 tablespoon ground turmeric

1 tablespoon ground cinnamon

1 tablespoon freshly ground black pepper

1 tablespoon ground cumin

1 tablespoon hot smoked paprika

1½ tablespoons fresh lemon juice

2½ pounds (1.15 kg) boneless, skinless chicken thighs, sliced into 1-inch (2.5 cm) strips

1 large white onion, cut into ¼-inch (6 mm) julienne

FOR SERVING

Pita bread and/or Bibb lettuce

Red cabbage, sliced

Torn cilantro, parsley, and mint

Harissa sauce

Scatter the chicken and onions evenly over the prepared sheet pans, being sure to not overcrowd the pans.

Roast until the chicken is cooked through and crispy around the edges, about 30 minutes.

To serve: Cut the top one-quarter off the pitas. Fill with the chicken, slather with some white sauce, and top with cabbage, torn herbs, and harissa. Serve immediately.

Dylan's
FOOLPROOF
CHICKEN PICCATA

SERVES 4 TO 6
PREP TIME: 20 MINUTES
COOK TIME: 15 MINUTES

6 thin-sliced chicken cutlets (about 1 pound/455 g total)

Kosher salt and freshly ground black pepper

Garlic powder

1 cup (120 g) all-purpose flour

¼ cup plus 1 tablespoon (75 ml) extra-virgin olive oil

¼ cup (40 g) capers, drained

5 cloves garlic, thinly sliced

¼ cup (60 ml) dry white wine

3 tablespoons fresh lemon juice

¼ cup (60 ml) chicken broth

2 tablespoons unsalted butter, at room temperature

SWAP OPTION

Since her son Calvin was diagnosed with celiac disease, Dylan now uses gluten-free bread crumbs in place of flour. It becomes more like a schnitzel situation, but there's nothing wrong with that.

Chicken breast isn't the most exciting thing in the world, but the Italian American trifecta of lemon, capers, and butter perks it right up. "This is hands-down my family's favorite dinner that I make," says Dylan. You're going to want to have some nice crusty bread on hand to sop up all of the bright, briny, buttery sauce. Or you could do what Dylan does and put baby spinach on the bottom of the serving platter, drizzle it with olive oil, season it with salt and pepper, add hot spaghetti straight from the pot to wilt the spinach, top with the chicken, and spoon over the sauce. Now that's a weeknight dinner.

Season both sides of each chicken cutlet with a generous sprinkling of salt, pepper, and garlic powder.

Place the flour in a shallow bowl with 1 teaspoon salt, ½ teaspoon pepper, and 1 teaspoon garlic powder and whisk until well combined.

Dredge each chicken cutlet in the flour mixture, shaking off any excess coating and transfer to a plate.

In a large skillet, warm ¼ cup (60 ml) of the olive oil over medium-high heat.

Working in batches to not crowd the pan, cook the chicken until lightly browned and cooked through, 2 to 3 minutes per side. Transfer to a clean plate and cover loosely with foil to keep warm.

Add the remaining 1 tablespoon olive oil to the skillet. Add the capers and garlic and cook, stirring constantly, until fragrant, 15 to 30 seconds. Add the wine and use a flat-bottomed wooden spoon to scrape up any browned bits from the bottom of the pan. Add the lemon juice and chicken broth and bring to a boil. Reduce the heat to low and simmer until slightly reduced, about 2 minutes.

Recipe continues

Remove from the heat, add the butter, and stir until melted. Taste and season with salt and pepper, if needed.

Dip both sides of the chicken in the sauce before transferring to a serving platter and drizzling the remaining sauce over the chicken. Serve immediately.

Curtis Stone's
BLACKENED SALMON WITH CREAMY CORN SAUTÉ

SERVES 4
PREP TIME: 15 MINUTES
COOK TIME: 20 MINUTES

FOR THE SALMON

2 teaspoons freshly ground black pepper

2 teaspoons flaky sea salt

2 teaspoons sweet paprika

½ teaspoon cayenne pepper

½ teaspoon celery seeds

½ teaspoon dried thyme

½ teaspoon garlic powder

4 skinless salmon fillets (6 ounces/170 g each)

1 tablespoon extra-virgin olive oil, plus more for coating the salmon

FOR THE CORN SAUTÉ

3 ears corn, husked

3 tablespoons butter

1 small yellow onion, diced

1 red bell pepper, diced

2 cloves garlic, finely chopped

½ cup (120 ml) reduced-sodium chicken stock

⅓ cup (80 ml) heavy cream

Kosher salt and freshly ground black pepper

1 tablespoon thinly sliced fresh chives

MAKE AHEAD

The spice mixture can be made up to 1 week ahead and stored airtight at room temperature.

To serve up summer on a plate, Curtis, chef at Maude in Beverly Hills, turns to Cajun flavors. He blackens the fish with paprika and cayenne to give it some sweet heat, and pairs it with a creamy corn sauté—a sort of maque choux—for even more sweetness. Fresh summer corn doesn't need much to shine, but this preparation certainly brings out its brilliance.

Cook the salmon: In a small bowl, mix together the black pepper, salt, paprika, cayenne, celery seed, thyme, and garlic powder to combine. Measure out 1 teaspoon and set aside.

Coat the salmon with olive oil and season with the remaining spice blend.

In a large skillet, warm 1 tablespoon olive oil over medium-high heat. Add the salmon and cook, turning halfway through, until well seared on both sides and the flesh is mostly opaque with a rosy center, about 3 minutes per side. Transfer to a serving platter to rest.

Meanwhile, make the corn sauté: Using a chef's knife, remove the kernels from the corn cobs and set aside. Using the back of the knife, scrape the cobs over a bowl to catch the corn pulp and milk. Set aside separately from the corn kernels.

In a large skillet, melt 2 tablespoons of the butter over medium-high heat. Add the onion, bell pepper, and reserved 1 teaspoon spice blend and cook, stirring occasionally, until softened, about 5 minutes.

Reduce the heat to medium, add the corn kernels and garlic, and cook, stirring occasionally, until the corn is tender, about 6 minutes.

Stir in the corn pulp, chicken stock, and cream and simmer for 2 to 3 minutes to reduce slightly. Remove from the heat and stir in the remaining 1 tablespoon butter. Season with salt and pepper, to taste.

Top the salmon with the corn sauté and garnish with the chives. Serve immediately.

Michael Solomonov's
COFFEE-BRAISED BRISKET

SERVES 4
PREP TIME: 30 MINUTES
COOK TIME: 5 HOURS
INACTIVE TIME: 36 HOURS

1 first-cut (flat cut) brisket (about 2½ pounds/1.15 kg)

1½ tablespoons kosher salt

1 tablespoon coarsely ground black pepper

¼ cup (60 ml) extra-virgin olive oil

2 large yellow onions, sliced

2 celery stalks, chopped

¼ cup (60 ml) tomato paste

½ cup (120 ml) brewed coffee

¼ cup (60 ml) pomegranate molasses

This is a three-generation brisket—and it's been tweaked every time it's been passed down. Michael's grandmother made hers with carrots, potatoes, and Heinz chili sauce, which gave it the traditional sweet and sour flavor. Her daughter, Michael's mother, added coffee for a rich and slightly bitter flavor. Michael's version keeps the coffee but swaps out the chili sauce for pomegranate molasses, a Middle Eastern condiment, which adds a sweet-tart flavor. It's a true family recipe from the chef and co-owner of Zahav in Philadelphia—and we're confident your family will love it, too.

Season the brisket on both sides with the salt and pepper. Cover loosely with plastic wrap and refrigerate overnight.

Preheat the oven to 350°F (180°C).

In a large skillet, warm the olive oil over medium heat. Add the onions and celery and cook, stirring occasionally, until softened but not caramelized, 12 to 15 minutes.

Add the tomato paste and cook, stirring occasionally, for 5 minutes.

Add the coffee and pomegranate molasses, bring the mixture to a simmer, then remove from the heat and stir to combine.

Place the brisket in a 9 by 13-inch (22 by 33 cm) casserole dish with a lid. Pour the sauce over the meat and cover tightly with a double layer of foil. Cover with the lid and bake until the meat is tender but not falling apart, 3 to 4 hours.

Let sit until the brisket is cool enough to handle, about 30 minutes.

Transfer the brisket to a cutting board and slice it thinly against the grain. Return the meat to the casserole dish, cover tightly with foil, and refrigerate overnight.

When ready to serve, preheat the oven to 300°F (150°C).

Bake until the brisket is warmed through, about 1 hour.

Plate the meat and spoon the sauce over the top.

Ching He Huang's
KUNG PAO EGGPLANT

SERVES 2
PREP TIME: 10 MINUTES
COOK TIME: 10 MINUTES

FOR THE KUNG PAO SAUCE

¾ cup plus 2 tablespoons (200 ml) cold vegetable stock

1 tablespoon Chinese light soy sauce

1 tablespoon ketchup

1 tablespoon Chinkiang black vinegar

1 tablespoon hoisin sauce

1 teaspoon garlic chili sauce

1 tablespoon Shaoxing wine

2 tablespoons cornstarch

FOR THE EGGPLANT

3 tablespoons canola oil

7 ounces (200 g) baby eggplants, sliced into ¼-inch (6 mm) fingers

2 cloves garlic, finely chopped

1 inch (2.5 cm) fresh ginger, peeled and finely grated

1 fresh medium red chile, seeded and finely chopped

2 dried red chiles

FOR SERVING

Steamed jasmine rice

1 large handful of roasted peanuts

2 large scallions, thinly sliced on the bias

Pinch of ground Sichuan pepper, toasted

SWAP OPTION

If you're not an eggplant person but still want to go the plant-based route, you can use chunky shiitake mushroom slices instead.

If you can kung pao chicken, why not eggplant? The popular Sichuan stir-fry dish is typically made with diced chicken, peanuts, and chile peppers, but in this vegan version, wok-charred eggplant cubes take the place of chicken. When tossed in the kung pao sauce, the velvety eggplant soaks up its flavors, becoming sticky, spicy, sweet, and sour. "It's a warming, comforting midweek meal in minutes," says TV chef and cookbook author Ching.

Make the kung pao sauce: In a medium bowl, whisk together the stock, soy sauce, ketchup, vinegar, hoisin, chili sauce, Shaoxing wine, and cornstarch until well combined. Set aside.

Prepare the eggplant: In a wok, heat 2 tablespoons of the oil over high heat until white wisps appear. Add the eggplant and stir-fry, tossing often, and adding up to ¼ cup (60 ml) water in small droplets around the rim of the wok to create steam, until softened, but still with a bite, and browned, 3 to 4 minutes. Transfer to a plate.

Add the remaining 1 tablespoon oil to the wok and add the garlic, ginger, fresh chile, and dried chiles and stir for a few seconds. Reduce the heat to medium, add the kung pao sauce, bring to a simmer, and cook until glossy, about 1 minute.

Add the eggplant and cook, stirring constantly, letting the sauce soak up, for 1 minute.

To serve: Plate the eggplant over a bed of steamed rice and garnish with peanuts, scallions, and Sichuan pepper. Serve immediately.

Edy Massih's
LEBANESE STUFFED ZUCCHINI WITH BROWN BUTTER PINE NUTS

SERVES 4
PREP TIME: 20 MINUTES
COOK TIME: 1 HOUR

2 tablespoons extra-virgin olive oil

2 medium yellow onions, finely diced

1 pound (455 g) ground beef (80/20)

1 tablespoon kosher salt

2½ tablespoons baharat spice blend

4 medium zucchini

1 (32-ounce/907 g) jar marinara sauce

2 teaspoons dried oregano

4 tablespoons (55 g) unsalted butter

½ cup (70 g) pine nuts

Steamed white rice, for serving

Chopped fresh parsley, for serving

Koussa mehshe—Lebanese stuffed zucchini—takes Edy, chef and owner of Edy's Grocer in Brooklyn, right back to his grandmother's blue-tiled kitchen, where he used to sit, mesmerized by her work and the love she poured into it. She'd carve out the flesh of each small green zucchini and stuff them with hashweh—a filling made of cooked ground beef, onion, baharat spice blend, pine nuts, and rice—then line them up in a pan, drown them with homemade tomato-oregano sauce, and bake them off until tender and steamy. Edy's deconstructed take on his grandmother's dish cuts the prep in half and adds brown butter pine nuts for a little added toastiness. Sahtein!

Preheat the oven to 400°F (200°C).

In a large skillet, warm the olive oil over medium-high heat. Add the onions and sauté, stirring frequently, until translucent, 6 to 7 minutes.

Add the beef and break it into small pieces with the back of a wooden spoon. Add the salt and 1½ tablespoons of the baharat and cook, stirring often and continuing to break down the beef, until cooked through, 7 to 8 minutes. Remove from the heat and set aside.

Halve the zucchini lengthwise and use a spoon to hollow out the centers of the zucchini, being careful to not pierce through the exterior. Transfer the flesh to a large bowl.

Using kitchen shears or your hands, break up the zucchini flesh into small bits. Add the marinara sauce. Add ¼ cup (60 ml) water to the marinara jar, cover, shake to grab any remaining sauce, and add it to the bowl. Add the oregano and remaining 1 tablespoon baharat and stir to combine.

Recipe continues

Spread half of the marinara mixture evenly over the bottom of a 9 by 13-inch (22 by 33 cm) baking dish,

Using the tines of a fork, poke some holes into the skin of the zucchini, being careful to keep them intact, and place them scooped side up, lining them up in the baking dish. Fill the cavities of the zucchini with the beef mixture, piling it on. Spoon the remaining marinara sauce evenly over the zucchini. Cover tightly with foil.

Bake for 20 minutes. Remove the foil and bake until the zucchini is tender and the sauce is bubbling, about 20 minutes.

Meanwhile, in a small saucepan, melt the butter over medium-low heat. Add the pine nuts and cook, stirring almost constantly, until the butter and pine nuts have browned, about 5 minutes.

To serve, plate the zucchini over a bed of rice with a scoop of sauce and garnish with the pine nuts and brown butter and a sprinkling of parsley.

David Rose's
ANCHO GRILLED SKIRT STEAK WITH CHIPOTLE CHIMICHURRI

SERVES 4
PREP TIME: 30 MINUTES
COOK TIME: 6 MINUTES
INACTIVE TIME: 12 HOURS
   25 MINUTES

FOR THE DRY RUB

1 tablespoon plus 1 teaspoon kosher salt

2 teaspoons ancho chile powder

2 tablespoons dried Mexican oregano

1 teaspoon freshly ground black pepper

1 teaspoon garlic powder

1 teaspoon onion powder

1 teaspoon ground cumin

FOR THE MARINATED STEAK

1½ pounds (680 g) skirt steak, excess fat removed

1 cup (240 ml) extra-virgin olive oil

¼ cup (60 ml) sherry vinegar

2 tablespoons dark brown sugar

¼ teaspoon red pepper flakes

¼ teaspoon kosher salt

¼ teaspoon freshly ground black pepper

1 tablespoon adobo sauce (from canned chipotles)

Juice of ½ lime

Ingredients continue

Growing up in New Jersey, David, author of *EGGin'*, developed a deep appreciation for Brazilian steakhouses—of which there are many in the state. So, one of his favorite ways to prepare skirt steak is in the churrasco style: marinating it in a flavorful sauce, grilling it, and serving it with chimichurri, the zingy, herb-packed sauce from Argentina. In his take on the dish, he travels north of South America—to Mexico—for some smokiness and subtle heat from ancho chiles and chipotles in adobo. "This is my ode to the mouthwatering flavors I was raised on," he says.

Make the dry rub: In a small bowl, mix together the salt, ancho powder, oregano, black pepper, garlic powder, onion powder, and cumin to combine.

Marinate the steak: Using paper towels, pat the steak dry. Season the steak liberally, on all sides, with the dry rub and let sit at room temperature for 20 minutes.

Meanwhile, in a medium bowl, whisk together the oil, vinegar, brown sugar, pepper flakes, salt, black pepper, adobo sauce, and lime juice to combine the marinade.

Place the steak into a large zip-top bag, pour the marinade over the top, seal the bag, and massage, making sure the steak is fully coated in the marinade. Refrigerate overnight.

Meanwhile, make the chimichurri: In a food processor, combine the cilantro, parsley, olive oil, vinegar, anchovy, lime juice, chipotles, adobo sauce, and garlic until smooth. Season with salt and black pepper to taste.

Recipe continues

FOR THE CHIMICHURRI

½ bunch cilantro, stem ends trimmed

½ bunch flat-leaf parsley, stem ends trimmed

¾ cup (180 ml) extra-virgin olive oil

2 tablespoons sherry vinegar

1 anchovy fillet

Juice of 1 lime

2 canned chipotle peppers, seeds removed

1 tablespoon adobo sauce (from canned chipotles)

1 clove garlic, smashed and peeled

Kosher salt and freshly ground black pepper

Preheat a grill to 450°F (235°C).

Remove the steak from the marinade, pat off any excess with paper towels, and let sit at room temperature for 20 minutes.

Grill the steak to medium-rare, about 3 minutes per side.

Transfer to a cutting board and let rest for 6 minutes. Slice the steak in half with the grain, then thinly slice with a knife held at an angle to the cutting board, against the grain.

Transfer to a serving platter and drizzle with the chimichurri. Serve immediately.

Marcus Samuelsson's
WHOLE ROAST JERK CHICKEN

SERVES 4
PREP TIME: 15 MINUTES
COOK TIME: 2 HOURS
INACTIVE TIME: 1 HOUR
**   10 MINUTES**

1 bunch fresh cilantro, stem ends trimmed and cut into large chunks

1 bunch scallions, root ends trimmed and cut into large chunks

1 cup (125 g) sliced fresh ginger

6 cloves garlic, peeled but whole

1 Scotch bonnet pepper, stemmed

1 cup (240 ml) soy sauce

1 cup (240 ml) fresh lime juice (from about 8 limes)

1 cup (200 g) packed light brown sugar

2 teaspoons ground allspice

1 cup (240 ml) extra-virgin olive oil

1 whole chicken (3½ pounds/ 1.6 kg)

2 cups (480 ml) chicken stock

As the saying goes, "If you love someone, roast them a chicken; if you *burn for* them, roast them a *jerk* chicken." We may or may not have just made up that saying, but we do believe it. A perfectly golden-skinned bird is a romantic gesture on its own, but adding Marcus's Jamaican jerk marinade—a tantalizing mixture of cilantro, scallions, ginger, garlic, Scotch bonnet pepper, soy sauce, lime juice, olive oil, brown sugar, and allspice—really heats things up. The best part about making a whole chicken, says the chef and owner of the Marcus Samuelsson Group, is "knowing how good the leftovers will be!"

In a large food processor, combine the cilantro, scallions, ginger, garlic, and Scotch bonnet and process until finely chopped. Add the soy sauce, lime juice, brown sugar, and allspice and process until smooth.

Transfer to a large bowl, add the oil, and whisk to combine.

Place the chicken into a large container and pour the marinade over it, making sure it's fully coated, and refrigerate for at least 1 hour or up to overnight.

Preheat the oven to 325°F (160°C).

Pour the stock into a roasting pan fitted with a rack.

Place the chicken onto the rack and bake until an instant-read thermometer registers 165°F (75°C) when inserted into the thickest part of the thigh, about 2 hours.

Rest for 10 minutes before slicing and serving.

Yasmin Fahr's
CITRUSY SEARED SCALLOPS

SERVES 4
PREP TIME: 15 MINUTES
COOK TIME: 10 MINUTES

2 tablespoons olive oil

1 pound (455 g) sea scallops, side muscles removed, patted dry

Kosher salt

1 small shallot, sliced into thin rings

½ cup (120 ml) dry white wine

1 tablespoon unsalted butter

1 tablespoon grated orange zest

¼ cup (60 ml) freshly squeezed orange juice

1 orange, peeled and cut into suprêmes

Chopped fresh flat-leaf parsley, for garnish

HOW TO SUPRÊME

1. Using a sharp knife, cut off the top and bottom of the citrus to create a flat bottom and expose the flesh.

2. In smooth strokes, following the curve of the flesh, remove the peel and pith, down to the flesh.

3. Once all the white pith has been removed, cut between the membranes of the flesh of the citrus to remove the membranes.

4. Squeeze the remaining juice from the flesh of the citrus on top of the segments.

When it comes to scallops, Yasmin wants us to think outside of the lemon box. Other citrus fruits—such as tangerines, mandarins, clementines, and navel oranges—are waiting patiently to bring out the sweetness of the buttery bivalve. The author of *Cook Simply, Live Fully* quickly sears the scallops in a super-hot pan, then uses white wine, butter, and citrus to create a bright and juicy sauce. The type of citrus you use is up to you, but crusty bread for soaking up the sauce is nonnegotiable.

Heat a 12-inch (30 cm) heavyweight skillet over medium-high heat until very hot, about 1½ minutes.

Add the oil and the scallops, season the tops with salt and cook until the scallops are opaque halfway up and they easily release from the pan, 2 to 3 minutes. Using tongs, transfer to a plate.

Add the shallots to the pan, season lightly with salt, and cook, stirring constantly, until softened but not browned, about 1 minute.

Add the white wine, use a wooden spoon to scrape up any browned bits from the pan, and cook until reduced by half, 2 to 3 minutes.

Add the butter, orange zest, and orange juice and stir until the butter is melted and emulsified, about 2 minutes.

Using tongs, return the scallops to the skillet, uncooked side down, and cook, basting the scallops with the cooking liquid, until cooked through, 1 to 2 minutes.

Transfer to a serving platter, top with the sauce, stagger the orange suprêmes around the scallops, and garnish with parsley. Serve immediately.

Matt Abdoo's
BOURBON & CHERRY GLAZED BABY BACK RIBS

SERVES 6
PREP TIME: 40 MINUTES
COOK TIME: 5 HOURS 10 MINUTES
INACTIVE TIME: 12 HOURS

FOR THE RUB

½ cup (100 g) dark brown sugar

¼ cup (50 g) granulated sugar

¼ cup (26 g) sweet paprika

2 tablespoons kosher salt

1 tablespoon freshly ground black pepper

1 tablespoon garlic powder

1 tablespoon onion powder

1 tablespoon mild chili powder

½ teaspoon ground cumin

½ teaspoon ground ginger

FOR THE BARBECUE SAUCE

2 cups (480 ml) ginger ale

1 cup (240 ml) ketchup

¾ cup (150 g) light brown sugar

½ cup (120 ml) cherry jam

⅓ cup (80 ml) bourbon

¼ cup (60 ml) distilled white vinegar

2 tablespoons grenadine

2 tablespoons honey

1½ teaspoons kosher salt

½ teaspoon freshly ground black pepper

¼ teaspoon onion powder

¼ teaspoon garlic powder

Ingredients continue

Matt, chef-partner at Pig Beach BBQ, was inspired to create this dish while sipping on a Manhattan. Bourbon and cherries—two ingredients central to the classic cocktail—would make a glorious glaze for a rack of ribs, he thought. The sweet and tart flavor of the cherries, plus the caramel and vanilla notes from the bourbon, pairs perfectly with the pork. Throw some ginger ale and grenadine in there, too, and you've got yourself a whole *bar*-becue. Get it? We'll see ourselves out—but not without one of these ribs.

Line your baking tray with foil before adding the wire rack to make cleanup easy.

Make the rub: In a small bowl, mix the dark brown sugar, granulated sugar, paprika, salt, pepper, garlic powder, onion powder, chili powder, cumin, and ginger until well combined. Set aside.

Make the barbecue sauce: In a 4-quart (3.8 L) saucepan, cook the ginger ale over medium-high heat until reduced by half, about 15 minutes.

Add the ketchup, light brown sugar, jam, bourbon, vinegar, grenadine, honey, salt, pepper, onion powder, and garlic powder and whisk to combine. Bring to a simmer, then reduce the heat to low and cook, stirring occasionally, until thickened, 35 to 40 minutes.

Carefully transfer the mixture to a blender and process until smooth. Transfer to an airtight container, cool to room temperature, then refrigerate until ready to use.

Cook the ribs: In a large nonreactive container, whisk together the ginger ale, bourbon, and grenadine until well combined. Add the ribs, cover in plastic wrap, and refrigerate overnight.

Remove the ribs from the marinade and transfer to a baking sheet fitted with a wire rack. Transfer some of the marinade to a spray bottle and reserve the remaining liquid.

Recipe continues

FOR THE RIBS

8½ cups (4 L) ginger ale

½ cup (120 ml) bourbon

¼ cup (60 ml) grenadine

2 racks baby back ribs
(2½ pounds/1.13 kg each)

4 tablespoons (55 g) unsalted
butter

Generously season the top and back sides of the ribs with the rub. Let sit at room temperature for 20 minutes.

Meanwhile, preheat a grill to 250°F (120°C).

Cook the ribs, spritzing with the reserved marinade every 20 minutes, for 3 hours.

Carefully and tightly wrap each rack of ribs in foil, adding 2 tablespoons of butter and ½ cup (120 ml) of the reserved marinade to each packet. Return to the grill and cook for 1 hour.

Carefully remove the ribs from the foil, generously brush the top side with the barbecue sauce, place them, bottom side down, on the grill and cook until the sauce is tacky, about 20 minutes.

Transfer to a cutting board and rest for 10 minutes before slicing into individual ribs and serving with additional barbecue sauce.

 TIP

Mop the ribs with the glaze during the last hour of cooking to get them all sticky and shiny.

The Grill Dads'
REVERSE-SEARED STUFFED BEEF TENDERLOIN

SERVES 6
PREP TIME: 25 MINUTES
COOK TIME: 2 HOURS
 40 MINUTES
INACTIVE TIME: 30 MINUTES

2 tablespoons fennel seeds

1 center-cut beef tenderloin (about 3½ pounds/1.6 kg), trimmed and silver skin removed

Kosher salt and freshly ground black pepper

Extra-virgin olive oil

8 cloves garlic, thinly sliced

1 teaspoon red pepper flakes

20 fresh basil leaves

6 slices prosciutto

8 slices Fontina cheese

Neutral oil

Flaky sea salt, such as Maldon

MAKE AHEAD

If you can, you should prepare this the day before you plan to serve it so the salt can really penetrate the beef. (It'll also mean less work for you on the day of your party.)

SWAP OPTION

Feel free to modify the stuffing ingredients to your liking (caramelized onions would be nice!), but avoid anything with a lot of moisture—you don't want a sogfest!

This roast from the Grill Dads, Ryan and Mark, is the showstopper of all showstoppers. When you cut into it to reveal its rosy pink interior and spiral of prosciutto, Fontina, basil, garlic, and fennel seeds, there will no doubt be "oohs" and "aahs" from your guests. Beef tenderloin is known for being super tender (hence its name) but not big on flavor. By butterflying and stuffing it, however, you create double the surface area for seasoning and pack it with savory goodies. In other words, you get the best of both worlds.

Preheat a grill to 200°F (95°C) with indirect heat.

In a small skillet, toast the fennel seeds over medium heat until fragrant, 1 to 2 minutes. Set aside to cool.

Meanwhile, with a short end of the tenderloin facing you, use a large chef's knife to make a cut ½ inch (13 mm) deep the length of the roast, starting about ½ inch (13 mm) up from the cutting board. As you cut, roll the roast open, while continuing to make shallow cuts and unrolling the roast as you go, until it is completely open and flat.

Cover with a sheet of plastic wrap and use the smooth side of a meat mallet to pound the roast to even it out and thin it slightly. Flip the roast over so that the smooth, original outside faces up and season it liberally with salt and pepper. Flip the roast back over and season the other side liberally with salt and pepper. Sprinkle the toasted fennel seeds evenly over the roast. Drizzle the roast with some olive oil.

Scatter the garlic, red pepper flakes, and all but 5 of the basil leaves evenly over the roast. Layer the prosciutto, then the Fontina, evenly over the roast. Roll the roast back up tightly, in the reverse order that you sliced it open so that it is back in its original shape.

Using kitchen twine, tie the roast in 5 spots, tight enough so that it makes small indentations in the meat.

Recipe continues

Add the roast, seam side up, to the grill and cook, covered, until the center of the roast reaches an internal temperature of 125°F (52°C). Remove the roast from the grill.

Increase the temperature of the grill to 550° (285°C) and allow to preheat for 10 to 15 minutes.

Meanwhile, brush the roast with some neutral oil.

Place the roast on the grill until seared, 3 to 5 minutes, and remove from the grill.

Rest the roast for 15 minutes before removing the twine and slicing the meat into 1-inch (2.5 cm) slices.

Transfer to a platter and serve with a drizzling of olive oil, some flaky sea salt, and the remaining basil.

JJ Johnson's
CAST-IRON PAELLA

SERVES 6
PREP TIME: 10 MINUTES
COOK TIME: 30 MINUTES

2 tablespoons grapeseed oil

4 boneless, skinless chicken thighs, cut into 1-inch (2.5 cm) pieces

Kosher salt

1 medium red onion, finely diced

4 cloves garlic, roughly chopped

2 cups (400 g) Valencia rice

1 Lady Hermit chile or other fresh chile, minced

½ teaspoon achiote powder

1½ teaspoons smoked paprika

1 teaspoon chili powder

1 cup (240 ml) dry white wine

3 cups (720 ml) chicken stock

½ pound (225 g) large shrimp (16/20), peeled and deveined

Freshly ground black pepper

½ cup (50 g) sliced okra

½ cup (45 g) sliced mini bell peppers

Paella might seem like one of those dishes you can only order at a restaurant, but it's actually easy to make at home, thanks to a trick JJ, chef and founder of Fieldtrip in New York City, learned from his grandmother. When her paella pan wouldn't fit on a small stove burner, she adapted by using a cast-iron skillet instead. The skillet evenly distributes heat, ensuring evenly cooked rice with a crispy bottom (called socarrat, pegao, or concón, depending on who you ask). It may not be prepared in a traditional manner, nor have traditional ingredients (we're looking at you, okra), but it'll take you on a journey from the sunny streets of Valencia to JJ's grandmother's similarly sunny kitchen.

In a 14-inch (35 cm) cast-iron skillet or paella pan, warm the oil over medium-high heat. Season the chicken with salt, add it to the pan, and sauté, stirring as needed, until partially cooked, about 3 minutes.

Push the chicken to one side of the pan. Add the onion and garlic to the other side and sauté until soft, about 2 minutes.

Add the rice, 1 teaspoon kosher salt, the fresh chile, achiote powder, ¾ teaspoon of the smoked paprika, and ½ teaspoon of the chili powder and toast, stirring all the ingredients, including the chicken, to combine. Let cook undisturbed for 1 to 2 minutes. Add the wine and cook, undisturbed, for 1 to 2 minutes.

Slowly add the stock and bring to a boil. Reduce the heat to a simmer and cook, undisturbed for 10 minutes.

Meanwhile, season the shrimp with salt, black pepper, the remaining ¾ teaspoon smoked paprika, and remaining ½ teaspoon chili powder.

Scatter the shrimp, okra, and mini bell peppers evenly over the rice, gently pressing them into the rice, and continue cooking until the shrimp is cooked through and the rice is tender, 10 to 12 minutes.

Serve immediately.

Laura Vitale's
BRAISED SHORT RIBS WITH GREMOLATA

SERVES 8
PREP TIME: 15 MINUTES
COOK TIME: 3 HOURS 20 MINUTES
INACTIVE TIME: 30 MINUTES

FOR THE SHORT RIBS

8 English-cut bone-in short ribs (each about 2 by 3 inches/5 by 7.5 cm)

Kosher salt and freshly ground black pepper

2 tablespoons avocado oil

1 large yellow onion, diced

6 cloves garlic, peeled but whole

½ cup (120 ml) tomato paste

3 cups (720 ml) dry red wine

2½ cups (590 ml) beef stock

2 large sprigs fresh thyme

FOR THE GREMOLATA

1 bunch flat-leaf parsley, finely chopped

2 cloves garlic, minced

2 anchovy fillets, finely chopped

Grated zest of ½ lemon

Kosher salt

This is one of those coveted low-effort, high-wow-factor dishes. It's Laura's go-to when she has a bunch of people coming over because she can assemble the gremolata—the vibrant condiment made with parsley, garlic, lemon zest, and anchovies—ahead of time and refrigerate it until ready to use. And the short ribs take mere minutes of hands-on prep. The dish just slowly simmers, which allows the author and host of *Laura in the Kitchen* to focus on spending time—and enjoying a couple glasses of wine—with her guests, rather than being stuck in the kitchen. The result is a deeply satisfying melt-in-your-mouth situation.

Prepare the short ribs: Preheat the oven to 325°F (160°C).

In a large Dutch oven, warm the oil over medium heat. Season all sides of the short ribs with salt and pepper. Working in batches, cook the short ribs until well seared on all sides, about 2 minutes per side. Transfer to a plate.

Pour out any rendered fat, leaving any browned bits behind. Add the avocado oil, onion, garlic, and a pinch of salt and cook, stirring often, until softened, about 4 minutes.

Add the tomato paste and cook, stirring constantly, for 30 seconds. Add the wine, stock, and thyme and stir to combine. Nestle the ribs into the pot, bone side up, cover with the lid, and transfer to the oven.

Bake until the meat is super tender and the bones easily pull away from the meat, about 3 hours.

Rest for 30 minutes.

Meanwhile, make the gremolata: In a small bowl, stir together the parsley, garlic, anchovies, lemon zest, and a pinch of salt to combine.

To serve, transfer the short ribs to a serving platter. Strain the cooking liquid into a fat separator. Once settled, pour the sauce over the short ribs. Discard the fat. Sprinkle the gremolata over the top and serve.

Sunny Anderson's
NACHO AVERAGE BURGER

SERVES 4
PREP TIME: 20 MINUTES
COOK TIME: 10 MINUTES
INACTIVE TIME: 1 HOUR

FOR THE PATTIES

1½ pounds (680 g) ground chuck (80/20)

1½ teaspoons kosher salt

1 teaspoon ground cumin

1 teaspoon ancho chile powder

Freshly ground black pepper

Extra-virgin olive oil, for drizzling

FOR THE PICO

2 plum tomatoes, seeded and finely chopped

1 medium jalapeño, seeded and finely chopped

½ medium red onion, finely chopped

1 teaspoon hot sauce, such as Cholula or Frank's RedHot

1 teaspoon fresh lime juice

Kosher salt and freshly ground black pepper

FOR THE SPREAD

¼ cup (60 ml) mayonnaise

¼ cup (60 ml) Mexican crema

2 canned chipotle peppers in adobo sauce, finely chopped

1 clove garlic, grated on a rasp-style grater

¼ teaspoon ground cumin

FOR ASSEMBLY

4 slices white American cheese

4 slices pepper Jack cheese

4 sesame rolls, halved and cut sides toasted on an oiled griddle

"If you come to my house, this is the burger I'm serving," says Sunny, who drew the inspiration for it from living in San Antonio, Texas, where big, beefy cookouts and Mexican flavors commonly converge. A quick pico de gallo is the perfect topping for a burger, as opposed to a lonely tomato slice, because you get the sweetness of the tomato along with the bite of red onion and fresh jalapeños. "I know purists like only salt and pepper in their burgers, but I'm not a purist," the co-host of *The Kitchen* says; she adds cumin and ancho chile powder to the mix. "I invite flavor to exist everywhere."

Make the patties: In a large bowl, break up the beef into small pieces. Sprinkle with the salt, cumin, ancho powder, and a few hefty grinds of black pepper. Using your nondominant hand, gently fold the meat over itself to combine. Do not overmix.

Divide the beef into 4 equal portions and gently shape each into a ball. Drizzle with olive oil, cover, and rest at room temperature for 1 hour.

Meanwhile, make the pico: In a medium bowl, gently toss together the tomatoes, jalapeño, red onion, hot sauce, lime juice, a pinch of salt, and a few grinds of black pepper to combine. Let rest alongside the burgers, tossing every so often.

Make the spread: In a small bowl, mix the mayonnaise, crema, chipotles, garlic, and cumin to combine. Refrigerate until ready to use.

Preheat a cast-iron griddle over medium heat.

To cook the burgers and assemble: Press each ball of beef into a patty slightly larger than the circumference of the rolls, place on the griddle, and cook until they easily release from the surface, about 4 minutes.

Flip the burgers and cook to your desired level of doneness. Add a slice of each cheese to each patty and cover with a large heat-resistant bowl until melted, about 1 minute.

To serve, smear a tablespoon of the spread over the bottom of the rolls, add the patties, and, using a slotted spoon, add a generous scoop of the pico over the cheese and add the top of the rolls. Serve immediately.

Radhi Devlukia's
TOFU TIKKA MASALA

SERVES 4
PREP TIME: 10 MINUTES
COOK TIME: 18 MINUTES

1 (14-ounce/397 g) package extra-firm tofu, patted dry and cut into ¾-inch (2 cm) cubes

1 teaspoon cornstarch

2 tablespoons curry powder

3 tablespoons butter

1 cup (70 g) roughly chopped cabbage

1 teaspoon salt

1 tablespoon garam masala

1 tablespoon chili powder

½ teaspoon ground turmeric

3 tablespoons tomato paste

1 (13.5-ounce/398 ml) can full-fat coconut milk

Cilantro leaves

Let's be real: We eat chicken tikka masala for the creamy, tangy, spice-packed sauce—not the chicken. So why not replace the meat with something that does an even better job at absorbing said sauce? The cubed tofu sucks it up like a sponge—a crispy sponge, though, as *JoyFull* author Radhi sears it until golden brown on all sides—while the tender cabbage picks up anything it may have missed.

In a medium bowl, toss the tofu with the cornstarch and 1 tablespoon of the curry powder to coat.

In a large sauté pan, melt 2 tablespoons of the butter over medium-high heat. Add the tofu and cook until crispy on all sides, 6 to 8 minutes. Transfer to a plate.

Add the remaining 1 tablespoon butter and the cabbage to the pan and stir to combine. Add the salt, garam masala, chili powder, turmeric, tomato paste, and remaining 1 tablespoon curry powder and toast, stirring constantly, for 2 minutes. Add the coconut milk, bring to a simmer, and cook until the cabbage is tender, about 4 minutes.

Add the tofu to the sauce, gently tossing until fully coated, and cook until the tofu is warmed through, 1 to 2 minutes. Serve immediately with a sprinkling of cilantro.

Katie Stilo's
SCENE DOCK SCHNITZEL

SERVES 4
PREP TIME: 15 MINUTES
COOK TIME: 25 MINUTES

1½ cups (180 g) all-purpose flour

Vegetable oil

2 tablespoons kosher salt

1 tablespoon garlic powder

1 tablespoon onion powder

1 cup (40 g) mini pretzels, crushed into fine crumbs

1 cup (85 g) panko bread crumbs

3 large eggs, beaten

4 boneless, skinless chicken breasts, butterflied and pounded to a ¼-inch (6 mm) thickness

Flaky sea salt

Honey mustard, for serving

Lemon wedges, for serving

If there's one thing our lead food stylist Katie is consistently whipping up in the scene dock, it's some kind of breaded cutlet. And, like with most things she makes backstage (see page 31 for her Apple Cider Doughnut Pancakes), she uses leftovers from cooking segments. In this case, there was extra chicken lying around and she wanted to coat it with something other than bread crumbs—something salty—and she spotted pretzels. That's how this pretzel-crusted schnitzel was born. When dipped in honey mustard, it tastes like those addictive pretzel pieces we like to grab for road trips—and the crew can't get enough. Everyone knows it's going to be a good day when Katie is frying up her cutlets.

Preheat the oven to 200°F (90°C).

Set up a dredging station in three large rimmed plates: In one plate, whisk the flour, salt, garlic powder, and onion powder until well combined. In a second, whisk the panko and pretzel crumbs until well combined and spread it evenly across the plate. Place the eggs in the third plate.

Line a sheet pan with a wire rack and set near the stove. In a large skillet, warm ¼ inch (6 mm) of oil over medium heat.

Working with one piece at a time, coat the chicken on both sides with the flour, shaking off any excess. Dip the chicken into the egg, coating it completely and allowing any excess to drip off. Coat the chicken in the panko/pretzel mixture, pressing it into the chicken and making sure it's well coated.

Carefully place the chicken into the skillet and cook until deep golden brown and cooked through, about 3 minutes per side. Transfer to the wire rack, sprinkle with some flaky sea salt, and keep warm in the oven. Repeat with the remaining chicken, adding more oil as needed.

Plate the chicken and serve with honey mustard and lemon wedges.

Erin French's
SMOKY TEA-BRINED TURKEY

SERVES 10
PREP TIME: 15 MINUTES
COOK TIME: 3 TO 3½ HOURS
INACTIVE TIME: 3 DAYS

¼ cup (15 g) smoky black tea, such as lapsang souchong

3 cups (410 g) kosher salt

3 cups (600 g) sugar

1 whole turkey (15 pounds/ 6.8 kg)

1 orange, quartered

4 onions, peeled and quartered

1 head garlic, cloves removed and peeled

2 bay leaves

1 cup (240 ml) apple cider

Extra-virgin olive oil

MAKE AHEAD
The brine can be made a day or two ahead of time and kept in the refrigerator.

Thanksgiving is a big deal on the show. It's the food team's Super Bowl. Every year, we invite a big group of our favorite chefs to share their top tips, techniques, and recipes ahead of the holiday. With dedicated segments in all three hours, it's a major production that we begin planning months in advance—long before you begin thawing your turkey.

So, with that in mind, we decided we had to include a turkey recipe—and not just any turkey recipe—one that many of us have made for our own families because it is that good. We've tried every type of marinade, but we keep coming back to this tea-based brine from Erin, the chef and owner of the Lost Kitchen. Lapsang souchong, a Chinese black tea that is dried over pinewood fire, imparts a smoky flavor into the bird—without smoking up the kitchen.

Prepare a sachet by placing the tea in a bit of cheesecloth and tying it with twine.

In a large stockpot, bring the salt, sugar, and 4 quarts (3.8 L) of cold water to a boil, stirring to dissolve.

Remove from the heat, add the tea sachet, and let cool completely. Remove the sachet and discard.

Transfer the brine to a large vessel, place the turkey into the brine, and add enough cool water to fully submerge the turkey. Cover and refrigerate for at least 24 hours and up to 36 hours.

Remove the turkey from the brine and place it, breast side up, on a wire rack set in a sheet pan. Refrigerate, uncovered, allowing the skin to dry out, for at least 12 hours, preferably overnight.

Remove the turkey from the refrigerator and let it come to room temperature, about 2 hours.

Preheat the oven to 350°F (180°C).

Recipe continues

Stuff the cavity of the turkey with the orange and as many of the onion wedges as will reasonably fit. Gently tuck the wings behind the body and using kitchen twine, tie the legs together to cinch up the cavity. Place the bird breast side up on a roasting rack in a roasting pan.

Add the remaining onion wedges to the bottom of the pan along with the garlic cloves and bay leaves. Add the cider and top with enough water so there is a good ¼ inch (6 mm) of liquid in the bottom of the pan.

Brush the turkey generously with olive oil and place in the preheated oven.

Monitor the turkey for perfect coloring, covering the bird with foil if overbrowning. Roast until an instant-read thermometer inserted into the thickest part of the thigh reaches 165°F (75°C) and the juices run clear, 3 to 3½ hours, depending on your oven and the size of your bird.

Remove from the oven and let rest, covered with foil, for at least 20 minutes before carving.

Al's
SPICE RACK RULES

SPICES

Cayenne pepper

Chile powder

Cinnamon, ground

Coriander, ground

Cumin, ground

Garlic powder

Onion powder

Paprika, sweet and smoked

Turmeric, ground

HERBS

Oregano, dried

Thyme, dried

Za'atar

Don't mess with Al's spice drawer.

Aside from their organization, he has other strict rules when it comes to his spices:

GO TO A SPICE SHOP. "In a pinch, your grocery store is great, but those things have been sitting there forever. Go to a good spice shop so you know when and where the spices originated."

BUY 4-OUNCE CONTAINERS. "That way, you'll use them up and they won't sit and lose potency with age."

USE THEM WITHIN 6 MONTHS. "You don't need all the spices in the world. Just buy the ones you'll use, and use them up before their flavor fades."

See the list at left for the carefully curated spices and dried herbs Al keeps in his spice drawer:

And with many of these spices, he creates a Greek-style seasoning blend—based loosely off the one from charcoal grill company Hasty Bake—that he puts on pork (see page 198), chicken, lamb, tuna, and more.

"Nothing annoys me as much as when my family members take spices out and put them back willy-nilly," **Al says.** "They are labeled and alphabetized for a reason."

AL'S GREEK-STYLE SPICE BLEND

MAKES ABOUT 1½ CUPS
PREP TIME: 5 MINUTES

½ cup (100 g) dark brown sugar

¼ cup (7 g) dried oregano

2 tablespoons smoked paprika

2 tablespoons kosher salt

1 tablespoon garlic powder

1 tablespoon onion powder

1 tablespoon paprika

1 tablespoon freshly ground
black pepper

1 tablespoon ground cumin

1 teaspoon ground cinnamon

1 teaspoon ground coriander

In a medium-sized bowl, mix the brown sugar, oregano, smoked paprika, salt, garlic powder, onion powder, paprika, pepper, cumin, cinnamon, and coriander, breaking up any lumps, until well combined.

Store in an airtight container for up to 1 month.

The Kicker:
DESSERTS

Of course, we had to end the show on a sweet note. Clearly, we're big on cakes—chocolate, carrot, chiffon, cheese, and even honey bun–inspired, each somewhere different on the spectrum of casual to celebratory. But we also love ourselves a little treat, so you'll find some grab-and-go goodies, too, like blondies, cookies (albeit *huge* ones from Jenna), and Hoda's mom's baklava.

Martha Stewart's
STRAWBERRIES & CREAM CHIFFON CAKE

SERVES 12
PREP TIME: 40 MINUTES
COOK TIME: 1 HOUR
INACTIVE TIME: 2 HOURS

FOR THE CAKE

2¼ cups (270 g) cake flour

1½ cups (300 g) sugar

2¼ teaspoons baking powder

¾ teaspoon salt

7 large egg yolks

½ cup (120 ml) safflower oil

¾ cup (180 ml) whole milk

9 large egg whites

½ teaspoon cream of tartar

2 teaspoons vanilla extract

FOR THE BERRIES AND CREAM

2 pounds (910 g) strawberries, hulled and halved or quartered (about 5 cups), plus more for serving

½ cup sugar

1 tablespoon fresh lemon juice

Pinch of salt

2 cups (480 ml) heavy cream

¼ cup (30 g) powdered sugar, plus more for sprinkling

A bowl of berries and cream is one of life's simplest pleasures. But when Martha wants to take simple to sumptuous, she turns the classic combo into a cake. This lighter-than-air chiffon cake will have you floating on a whipped-cream cloud while being hand-fed fresh strawberries. In other words, Martha says, it's "what summer dreams are made of."

Make the cake: Preheat the oven to 325°F (160°C).

In a large bowl, whisk together the flour, ¾ cup (150 g) of the sugar, the baking powder, and salt until well combined.

In another large bowl, whisk the egg yolks until smooth. Add the oil and milk and whisk to combine. Add the flour mixture and whisk until just combined.

In a stand mixer fitted with the whisk, beat the egg whites over high speed until frothy, about 1 minute. Add the cream of tartar and vanilla and beat until soft peaks form, 1 to 2 minutes. With the machine running, continue beating the egg whites while gradually adding the remaining ¾ cup (150 g) sugar until stiff, glossy peaks form, about 4 minutes.

Add one-third of the egg white mixture to the cake batter and whisk to combine. Add the remaining egg whites and gently fold them into the batter until thoroughly combined.

Pour the batter into a 10-inch (25 cm) tube pan, filling it up two-thirds of the way to the top (there may be leftover batter), gently spread it evenly across the pan, and bake until set and the top of the cake springs back when touched, about 1 hour.

Cool upside down (or over a bottle) for 1 hour.

Meanwhile, make the berries and cream: In a large bowl, gently toss the strawberries, sugar, lemon juice, and salt to combine. Let macerate, stirring occasionally, for 1 hour.

Recipe continues

Slide a paring knife around the edges of the cake pan to help release the cake. Remove it from the pan.

Using a large serrated knife, slice the cake, horizontally, into three even layers.

In a stand mixer fitted with the whisk, whip the cream and powdered sugar to medium peaks.

Place the bottom layer of the cake onto a serving plate or cake stand. Spread half of the berry mixture, including the juices, evenly over the cake. Spread half of the whipped cream evenly over the berries. Top with the middle layer and repeat another layer of the berries and whipped cream. Place the remaining cake layer over the top and refrigerate for 1 hour.

Sprinkle with powdered sugar and serve with additional strawberries.

Maya-Camille Broussard's
BLACK CITRUS CAKE

SERVES 12
PREP TIME: 30 MINUTES
COOK TIME: 1 HOUR 30 MINUTES
INACTIVE TIME: 1 HOUR (FOR COOLING)

FOR THE CAKE

Softened butter and cocoa powder, for the pan

2½ cups (300 g) unbleached all-purpose flour

¾ cup (75 g) black cocoa powder

2 teaspoons kosher salt

1 pound (455 g) unsalted butter, at room temperature

3 cups (600 g) sugar

5 large eggs, at room temperature

3 large egg yolks, at room temperature

¼ cup (60 ml) orange liqueur

1 teaspoon vanilla extract

Grated zest of 1 orange

FOR THE GANACHE

½ cup (75 g) finely chopped dark chocolate

½ cup (75 g) finely chopped milk chocolate

⅔ cup (160 ml) heavy whipping cream

2 tablespoons orange liqueur

2 teaspoons orange extract

Grated zest of 1 orange, for garnish

This cake is a chocolate lover's dream. Using black cocoa in the cake, and both dark and milk chocolate in the ganache, Maya-Camille, author of *Justice of the Pies* and chef and owner of the bakery of the same name in Chicago, creates a deeply and richly satisfying dessert. And since orange and chocolate are a match made in heaven, she adds orange liqueur, extract, and zest as a bright accompaniment to the earthiness of the cocoa. It may be dark as coal, but this cake shines like a diamond.

Make the cake: Grease a 10- to 12-inch (25 to 30.5 cm) Bundt pan with butter and dust with dark cocoa powder. Set aside.

In a bowl, whisk the together flour, black cocoa, and salt until well combined.

In a stand mixer fitted with the paddle, cream the butter and sugar, scraping the sides of the bowl as needed, until light and fluffy, about 10 minutes.

Add the eggs one at a time, allowing each to fully incorporate before adding the next. Add the yolks, orange liqueur, vanilla, and orange zest and mix to combine. Add the flour mixture and mix, scraping the sides of the bowl as needed, until just combined.

Pour the batter into the prepared pan and gently tap the pan to level out the batter and remove any air bubbles.

Place the cake into a cold oven, then set the temperature to 300°F (150°C) and bake until a cake tester comes out clean when inserted into the center of the cake, about 1 hour 30 minutes.

Let cool in the pan for 30 minutes, then invert onto a wire rack to cool completely.

Recipe continues

Make the ganache: Place both chocolates in a heatproof medium bowl.

In a small saucepan, heat the cream over medium heat until it steams. Pour the hot cream over the chocolate, cover with plastic wrap, and let sit for 5 minutes.

Uncover and whisk the chocolate and cream until smooth. Add the orange liqueur and orange extract and whisk to combine.

Transfer the cake to a serving platter or cake stand and pour the ganache evenly over the top and garnish with the orange zest.

Savannah's
ANY-COOKIE-CRUST CHEESECAKE

SERVES 10
PREP TIME: 20 MINUTES
INACTIVE TIME: 10 HOURS

FOR THE CRUST

2½ cups (240 g) graham cracker crumbs

¼ cup (50 g) sugar

1 stick (4 ounces/115 g) unsalted butter, melted

FOR THE FILLING

3 (8-ounce/226 g) packages cream cheese, room temperature

1¼ cups (155 g) powdered sugar

1 teaspoon vanilla bean paste

1 teaspoon vanilla extract

½ teaspoon kosher salt

2 (8-ounce/226 g) containers whipped topping, such as Cool Whip, thawed

FOR THE BERRY TOPPING

4 cups mixed berries, such as strawberries, blackberries, raspberries, and blueberries

½ cup (100 g) sugar

 TIP

Use a dry measuring cup to help guide the crumbs evenly up the sides of the springform pan.

"Dessert is my favorite meal," says Savannah. "A lot of times, dinner is just a precursor to get out of the way to get to dessert—especially if that dessert is cheesecake." Her cheesecake is about as easy as it gets; it's no-bake (perfect for the warmer months when the oven is off-limits), and you can customize it with the cookie or cracker of your choice (Savannah usually goes for graham crackers or Oreos). You could make it even easier with a premade crust, but she insists it's much more fun to enlist the kids to smash the crackers or cookies in a zip-top bag. You'll be rewarded with a cheesecake that is velvety, light, fluffy, and, perhaps most important, not too sweet.

Make the crust: In a medium bowl, stir the graham cracker crumbs, sugar, and melted butter until the mixture resembles wet sand.

In a 9-inch (22 cm) springform pan, using your fingers, press the crumbs evenly along the bottom and 2 inches (5 cm) up the sides of the pan to create a crust. Set aside.

Make the filling: In a stand mixer fitted with the paddle, beat the cream cheese, powdered sugar, vanilla bean paste, vanilla extract, and salt, scraping the sides of the bowl often, until fluffy, about 3 minutes.

Using a silicone spatula, fold in the whipped topping to combine.

Pour the filling into the prepared crust, using an offset spatula to level off the top. Transfer to the freezer and freeze for at least 6 hours, or up to overnight.

Remove the sides of the springform pan, then place the cheesecake in the refrigerator to thaw, for at least 4 hours.

Make the berry topping: In a large bowl, toss the berries and sugar to combine. Let sit for 30 minutes, tossing every so often.

To serve, slice the cheesecake and serve with a generous spoonful of the berry topping.

Gesine Bullock-Prado's
DOUBLE-CRUMBLE APPLE CRISP

SERVES 6
PREP TIME: 35 MINUTES
COOK TIME: 50 MINUTES

FOR THE CRUMBLE

5 cups (600 g) all-purpose flour

1 cup (220 g) packed light brown sugar

1 cup (200 g) granulated sugar

1 teaspoon ground cinnamon

½ teaspoon salt

¼ teaspoon ground nutmeg

1 pound (455 g) unsalted butter, melted

FOR THE FILLING

5 tart medium baking apples, such as Granny Smith

⅓ cup (75 g) packed light brown sugar

Grated zest and juice 1 lemon

1 tablespoon cornstarch

½ teaspoon ground cinnamon

Pinch of ground nutmeg

Pinch of salt

Vanilla ice cream, for serving

 TIP

If you have extra crumble, it freezes really well and can be used as a streusel on everything from muffins to future pies.

In Gesine's family, apple crisp has one (perhaps controversial) rule: no oats. If they're going to have dessert, nothing is allowed to get in the way of the butter and sugar. Apples are already healthy enough, says the owner and baking instructor at Sugar Glider Kitchen in Vermont, so the crumble should be pure, unadulterated decadence. In this case, the crumble conveniently acts as both the bottom crust *and* the crispy topping—meaning double the decadence.

Preheat the oven to 350°F (180°C). Coat a 9 by 13-inch (22 by 33 cm) quarter-sheet pan with cooking spray.

Make the crumble: In a large bowl, whisk together the flour, brown sugar, granulated sugar, cinnamon, salt, and nutmeg to combine. Add the melted butter and use a wooden spoon to gently mix until small clumps form.

Press a little more than half of the mixture into the prepared sheet pan.

Bake until the crust is just starting to get golden brown on top, about 15 minutes.

Meanwhile, make the filling: Line a 13 by 18-inch (33 by 45 cm) half-sheet pan with a wire rack.

Peel and core the apples. Halve the apples, then cut each half into 8 slices. Scatter the apples evenly over the cooling rack and bake for 5 minutes.

Meanwhile, in a large bowl, stir together the brown sugar, lemon zest, lemon juice, cornstarch, cinnamon, nutmeg, and salt to combine.

Add the parbaked apples and toss to combine.

Layer the apples onto the crust, overlapping, in rows. Sprinkle the remaining crumble evenly over the top.

Bake until the crumble is golden brown, 25 to 30 minutes.

Serve with ice cream.

Debbie Cohen Kosofsky's
FORGET-THE-FROSTING CARROT CAKE

SERVES 12
PREP TIME: 20 MINUTES
COOK TIME: 45 MINUTES

2 cups (240 g) all-purpose flour

2 teaspoons baking powder

½ teaspoon baking soda

1 tablespoon ground cinnamon

1 teaspoon kosher salt

3 large eggs, at room temperature

1⅓ cups (320 ml) vegetable oil

2 teaspoons vanilla extract

1½ cups (300 g) sugar

3 cups (315 g) grated carrots

½ cup (60 g) finely chopped walnuts

While in high school, our senior producer Debbie developed a carrot cake recipe so good, she convinced her parents to turn their kitchen into a professional-grade bakery so she could sell it. She got one order—from her dad: two hundred carrot cakes to be given out as a corporate holiday gift. Her mother helped her peel carrots until their hands turned orange. That experience sealed Debbie's entrepreneurial fate: She never wanted to see another carrot and closed up shop. But she did end up picking up the peeler again—and she still bakes them in small tins to give out as gifts to this day. Debbie swears this carrot cake is so moist, it doesn't need any frosting, but you can always add it if you feel so inclined.

Preheat the oven to 350°F (180°C). Coat two 8½ by 4-inch (20 by 10 cm) loaf pans with cooking spray.

In a large bowl, whisk together the flour, baking powder, baking soda, and cinnamon until well combined.

In another large bowl, beat the eggs until smooth. Add the vegetable oil and vanilla and whisk to combine. Add the sugar and whisk to combine. Add the flour mixture and whisk until just combined. Add the carrots and walnuts and stir to combine. Divide the batter evenly between the prepared pans.

Bake until a toothpick comes out clean when inserted into the center of the cake, about 50 minutes. Transfer to a wire cooling rack to cool completely.

Christina Tosi's
BLUEBERRIES & CREAM BLONDIES

MAKES 9 BARS
PREP TIME: 15 MINUTES
COOK TIME: 40 MINUTES
INACTIVE TIME: 1 HOUR
**   30 MINUTES (COOLING)**

1 stick (4 ounces/115 g) unsalted butter

⅓ cup (55 g) plus ¾ cup (125 g) white chocolate chips,

⅔ cup (135 g) granulated sugar

¼ cup (55 g) light brown sugar

1 large egg, at room temperature

1 teaspoon clear vanilla extract

¾ cup plus 1 tablespoon (98 g) all-purpose flour

½ teaspoon kosher salt

½ cup (85 g) dried blueberries

SWAP OPTIONS

Add 1 teaspoon lemon extract to zing it up. Swap dried cranberries or raisins for the blueberries. Add 1½ teaspoons ground cinnamon. Swap butterscotch chips for the white chocolate chips—the world is your blondie!

These dense and fudgy, sugar cookie–esque bar cookies may sound super summery—and they are, in fact, delightful in the summer—but because they use dried blueberries, you can make them year-round. Chef and founder of the Milk Bar restaurant chain, Christina was inspired to create these blondies by the blueberry muffin top—aka the crown jewel of the muffin—with its golden brown, slightly crispy exterior and moist, blueberry-studded interior. We'll take this as permission—nay, encouragement—to enjoy them for breakfast paired with a hot cup of coffee.

Preheat the oven to 325°F (160°C).

Line an 8 by 8-inch (20 by 20 cm) square baking dish with heavy-duty foil, leaving a couple of inches of overhang on each side, and spray with cooking spray.

In a large microwave-safe bowl, heat the butter and ⅓ cup (55 g) of the white chocolate in 30-second intervals, stirring after each, until fully melted. Mix until smooth.

Add the granulated sugar and brown sugar and mix to combine. Add the egg and vanilla and mix, scraping down the sides of the bowl, until well combined. Add the flour and salt and mix just until combined.

Spread the batter evenly across the surface of the prepared baking dish. Scatter the dried blueberries and the remaining ¾ cup (125 g) white chocolate chips evenly over the surface of the blondie batter. Use a table knife to swirl some of the toppings into the batter, being sure to leave some exposed on top.

Bake until the edges are golden brown and the center is set, about 40 minutes.

Let cool to room temperature in the pan. Using the overhanging foil, carefully lift the blondies out of the pan. Cut into 9 squares and store in an airtight container at room temperature for up to 5 days or in the refrigerator for up to 2 weeks.

Jocelyn Delk Adams's
HONEY BUN CAKE

SERVES 24
PREP TIME: 15 MINUTES
COOK TIME: 25 MINUTES
INACTIVE TIME: 20 MINUTES

FOR THE CAKE

1 (15.25-ounce/430 g) box yellow cake mix

1 cup (240 ml) sour cream

¾ cup (180 ml) vegetable oil

4 large eggs

2 teaspoons vanilla extract

1 cup (210 g) packed light brown sugar

2 teaspoons ground cinnamon

¼ teaspoon ground nutmeg

FOR THE ICING

1½ cups (180 g) powdered sugar

¼ cup (60 ml) whole milk

1 teaspoon vanilla extract

Close your eyes and imagine you're a kid again. You just got your allowance, so you run to your local convenience store and pick up a honey bun. You open the wrapper and are greeted by the scent of cinnamon and the sight of its sticky glaze. Now, back in the present, imagine that feeling—but in cake form. Made with cake mix, author and founder of Grandbaby Cakes Jocelyn's nostalgic creation can be prepped in just 20 minutes and is sure to bring all those sweet memories rushing right back—no trip to the corner store needed.

Make the cake: Preheat the oven to 350°F (180°C). Spray a 9 by 13-inch (23 by 33 cm) baking pan with cooking spray.

In a large bowl, whisk together the cake mix, sour cream, oil, eggs, and vanilla until well combined.

Pour half of the batter into the prepared baking pan and, using an offset spatula, spread it evenly across the pan.

In a small bowl, mix the light brown sugar, cinnamon, and nutmeg to combine, then sprinkle it evenly over the cake batter.

Pour the remaining batter over the sugar/spice mixture and, using an offset spatula, spread it as evenly as possible across the pan. Using an offset spatula or table knife, run it through the batter to create swirls of cake and brown sugar filling.

Bake until a toothpick comes out clean when inserted into the center of the cake, 25 to 30 minutes.

Meanwhile, make the icing: In a medium bowl, whisk together the powdered sugar, milk, and vanilla until smooth.

Pour the icing over the warm cake, spread it evenly over the top and let sit until set, about 20 minutes.

Serve warm or at room temperature.

Jenna's
COWBOY COOKIES

MAKES 16 LARGE COOKIES
PREP TIME: 20 MINUTES
COOK TIME: 20 MINUTES (PER BATCH)

1½ cups (180 g) all-purpose flour

1½ teaspoons baking powder

1½ teaspoons baking soda

1½ teaspoons ground cinnamon

½ teaspoon kosher salt

1½ sticks (6 ounces/170 g) unsalted butter, at room temperature

½ cup plus 2 tablespoons (125 g) granulated sugar

¾ cup plus 2 tablespoons (180 g) packed light brown sugar

1 large egg, at room temperature

1 large egg yolk, at room temperature

1½ teaspoons vanilla extract

1½ cups (250 g) semisweet chocolate chips

1½ cups (145 g) old-fashioned rolled oats

1 cup (105 g) sweetened coconut flakes

1 cup (110 g) chopped pecans

These cookies are very Texas. They're massive and studded with so many mix-ins: chocolate chips, oats, coconut flakes, and pecans. Laura Bush put them on the map during her husband's first presidential campaign, but she was making them for her kids well before that. Jenna loves them for their "Texan hardiness," she says. "They capture the spirit of where I'm from." To make them a little more moist, Jenna adds an extra egg yolk to the recipe. But she keeps the cinnamon, of course—that's what really lassos everything together.

Preheat the oven to 350° F (180°C). Line two sheet pans with parchment paper.

In a large bowl, whisk together the flour, baking powder, baking soda, cinnamon, and salt until well combined.

In a stand mixer fitted with the paddle, beat the butter until smooth and creamy, 1 to 2 minutes. Add the granulated sugar and brown sugar and beat until creamy, scraping down the bottom and sides of the bowl as needed, 3 to 4 minutes. Add the whole egg, egg yolk, and vanilla and mix until well combined, about 1 minute. Add the flour mixture and mix until just combined. Add the chocolate chips, oats, coconut, and pecans and stir until just combined.

Using a ¼-cup (60 ml) cookie scoop, portion the dough and drop onto the lined sheet pans, spacing the mounds at least 2½ inches (6 cm) apart and from the rim of the baking pan to allow for spreading.

Bake in batches, until the edges are lightly browned, 17 to 20 minutes, rotating the sheet pan front to back halfway through.

Let sit on the sheet pan for 5 minutes before transferring to a wire rack to cool completely.

HONEY-SOAKED BAKLAVA

MAKES 48 PIECES
PREP TIME: 35 MINUTES
COOK TIME: 1 HOUR 15 MINUTES
**INACTIVE TIME: AT LEAST 4
    HOURS (FOR COOLING)**

FOR THE SYRUP

½ cup (100 g) sugar

½ cup (120 ml) honey

1 teaspoon vanilla extract

FOR THE FILLING

6 cups (600 g) walnuts, chopped
into small pieces

1 cup (200 g) sugar

2 tablespoons unsalted butter,
melted and cooled

FOR ASSEMBLY

1 (16-ounce/455 g) package phyllo
dough, thawed and brought to
room temperature

2 sticks (8 ounces/225 g)
unsalted butter, melted

TIP

Keep the phyllo dough covered
when you're not using it, so it
doesn't dry out. Pour the cool
syrup over the baklava as soon as
it comes out of the oven so that
the phyllo stays crispy.

This recipe is a labor—with many, many layers—of love. Sweet, nutty, syrupy, and flaky, Hoda's mom Sami's baklava defines her childhood. "I can remember, ever since I was little, walking into the kitchen and watching her meticulously lay out the layers of that phyllo dough," she says. "It was mesmerizing to me." When Hoda first started working at *TODAY*, her mom said, "I'm going to make it for everybody," and to this day, Hoda will still bring a tub of her mom's baklava into the control room at five in the morning and put one on everyone's desk. Sami will always ask her, "Did they like it?" and the answer is always a resounding "Yes."

Preheat the oven to 325°F (160°C).

Make the syrup: In a small saucepan, whisk together the sugar, honey, vanilla, and 1 cup (240 ml) cold water. Heat over medium-high heat until the sugar has completely dissolved, about 3 minutes. Transfer to a bowl and refrigerate to cool.

Make the filling: In a large bowl, mix the walnuts, sugar, melted butter, and 2 tablespoons (30 ml) of cold water, adding a splash more water, as needed, until well combined and the consistency of barely moist sand.

To assemble: Unfold the phyllo dough, place on a clean work surface, and trim it to fit a 9 by 13-inch (23 by 33 cm) baking pan. Discard the trimmings and cover the phyllo sheets with a clean kitchen towel.

Brush the baking pan with some of the melted butter. Begin layering the phyllo dough sheets in the prepared baking pan, brushing each sheet with a layer of butter before adding the next, using one-third of the sheets.

Spread half of the walnut filling evenly over the phyllo sheets.

Repeat with a second layer of buttered phyllo, using another one-third of the sheets. Top with the remaining walnut filling. Add the remaining phyllo dough sheets, brushing each with butter and drizzling any remaining butter evenly over the top.

Recipe continues

Using a serrated knife, score a diamond shape pattern across the baklava, cutting no deeper than halfway through.

Bake until golden brown, about 1 hour 15 minutes.

Carefully drizzle the cooled syrup over the top of the baklava and, using an offset spatula spread it evenly over the top, allowing it to drizzle through all the cuts. Use a serrated knife to complete the diamond shape by cutting all the way through. Let cool to room temperature, at least 4 hours or up to overnight.

Store, covered tightly with plastic wrap, at room temperature for up to 5 days.

ACKNOWLEDGMENTS

HERE AT TODAY, AS YOU KNOW BY NOW, food is one of the special ingredients of the show. And what better way to celebrate that than with a cookbook? This has been an exciting and fulfilling project, made possible by a big team. There are many talented people who work on the show's food segments, but here, I want to recognize those who specifically contributed to this book.

A huge thank-you to Libby Leist, executive vice president, and Tom Mazzarelli, executive producer, for the support and encouragement to pursue this idea.

Starting at the beginning, thank you to Emma Lux, a former booker, who helped get this cookbook off the ground.

Holly Dolce, our editor at Abrams, wholeheartedly embraced the idea. Your enthusiastic guidance has been a shining force. Also at ABRAMS: Diane Shaw and Danielle Youngsmith, thank you for your artistic direction, and thank you to Hannah Braden, Lisa Silverman, and Peggy Garry.

What made this project so special, above all, was the unwavering support of Savannah, Hoda, Craig, Al, Carson, Sheinelle, Dylan, and Jenna: Your enthusiasm, ideas, recipes, and stories truly enhanced this project from the get-go.

A big shout-out to the celebrity chefs and cooks who so often grace our studio and were truly excited to be a part of this cookbook. You are the foundation of TODAY Food.

Thank you, Anna Magliocco, NBC's senior vice president of digital growth, for launching the cookbook with us.

Once the project was greenlit, a small, tight-knit team of four was assembled: Emi, Katie, Savannah, and myself.

Hats off to Emi Boscamp, senior food editor, who stepped away from Today.com to focus on writing this book. Your approachable style and keen grasp of what we're all looking for in a recipe grace every page.

To Katie Stilo, food stylist and culinary producer, thank you for your dedication to both worlds, balancing your time and energy between the cookbook and the studio kitchen. Your top-rated culinary skills have never been more evident.

Savannah Smith took on the role of project manager, seamlessly juggling the multitude of details. Thank you for continuously moving things toward the finish line.

Amy Wolf and Nikki Mondschein, the show's legal counsel, provided guidance every step of the way. To the finance unit, Jenny Green, Vanessa Rowson, and Michael Triplett, thank you for assisting with the budget. To the digital team, Ashley Codianni, Arianna Davis, and Margaret O'Malley, and office manager Elizabeth Laskie, thank you for your support.

Thanks to Evan Klupt, our go-to for logistical issues, for arranging studio space to photograph the book at NBC's Long Island City field operations building. We were welcomed by Stacy Brady, Marc Weinstock, Danny Miller, J. P. Park, Jonathan Jackson, Martha Rosero, Gazmend Belega, and volunteer hand models Eli Brown and Miguel Toran.

Neal Carter, senior producer of graphics, along with art director Paul Maccarone, your invaluable input was very much appreciated. Pete Breen, senior broadcast producer, provided helpful editorial input.

Booking producer Abby Russ and executive assistants Madeleine Merritts and Bonnie Bering led the coordinated effort of contacting the chefs.

With appreciation for the talent executive assistants who helped coordinate the many meetings and photo shoots: in alphabetical order, Jacqueline Agnolet, Laurie Brandt, Mary Casalino, Bailey Coronis, Julia Plant, Kaitlin Vickery, and Briana Watson.

Thank you to Ed Helbig, head of design, along with Laura Zarn and Elike Bargas, who organized the multitude of props needed for the photography shoots. The prop team, led by Brianne Demmler and assisted by Jennifer Chavez, Jean-Marc Claude Solak, Barbara Baker-Peña, Aiden DiMaio, Patti Flynn, and Heidi Hernandez, helped procure the many items for the dozens of recipes.

Every recipe was tested by food stylists Anthony Contrino and Carrie Parente. Thank you for your perseverance.

The back kitchen team, coordinated and led by Katie, tirelessly helped out on set. To Anthony, Lish Steiling, Dawn Miller, Kenny Spooner, Charlie Falotico, Alison Lee, and Tori Keefe, thank you for bringing your talent and good cheer to the LIC kitchen. To the scene dock team, Namrata Hegde and Krissy Downey, kudos for keeping the engine running in Studio 1A.

The creative prop selection for every dish was the work of artistic stylist Anduin Havens. The thought and care put into every detail was greatly appreciated.

There are two photographers who shaped this book. To Nathan Congleton, senior studio photographer, thank you for finding the fleeting moments to capture the studio shots. Your candid photos are a reflection of that. Johnny Miller, your recipe photographs mesmerized us from the first click. Your beautiful work is stamped on every page.

The chef glossary was organized with the help of Katie Avebe, Mish Coffey, Veronica Manley, and Lizzy Yee.

The coordination of choosing and collecting recipes from our contributing chefs was made possible by their teams. In alphabetical order, a big thanks to Dagne Aiken, Sonia Armstead, Katie-Jane (KJ) Arthur, Carrie Bachman, Michelle Brandabur, Rochelle Brown, Gee Burns, Julie Ceresnie, Michael Dutton, Diandra Escamilla, Stephanie Francis, Laryl Garcia, David Gruber,

Tara Halper, Kate Heather, Sarah Hemalyn, Standish Hicks, Sally Jackson, Kim Kaminsky, Jami Kandel, Juliet Kapanjie, Jaret Keller, Elyse King, Alexa Levin, Chloe Mata Crane, Helen Medvedovsky, Tara Melega, Elise Merghart, Sarah New, Willie Norkin, Andrea Jackson Ott, Rochelle Palermo, Becca Parrish, Alexy Posner, Amanda Quintal, Hannah Randle, Elise Reinemann, Katie Reisert, John Rice, Rémy Robert, Elena Rodriguez-Villa, Christine Sanchez, Lauren Sklar, Jennifer Sommer, Brie Sosnov, Andrea Soto, Karly Stillman, Jonah Straus, Kelly Taylor, Kate Tyler, Lysbett Valles, Sarah Virden, and Ali Wald. An additional thanks to Rob Magnotta for your help coordinating Johnny's photo shoot.

Last, but certainly not least, heartfelt thanks to Ina Garten, who graciously agreed to write the foreword. Your warmth, loyalty, and extraordinary talent continue to enamor us.

This cookbook has been a labor of love. We hope our shared passion and joy leap off these pages. TODAY will be right there with you as you cook, one recipe at a time.

—Debbie Cohen Kosofsky,
senior producer

CONTRIBUTORS

Thank you to this all-star roster of contributors who regularly bring TODAY Food to life in our studio, in alphabetical order:

MATT ABDOO

CAMILA ALVES MCCONAUGHEY

SUNNY ANDERSON

JOSÉ ANDRÉS

DANIEL BOULUD

MAYA-CAMILLE BROUSSARD

GESINE BULLOCK-PRADO

GABY DALKIN

SIRI DALY

JOCELYN DELK ADAMS

RADHI DEVLUKIA

YASMIN FAHR

BOBBY FLAY

ERIN FRENCH

INA GARTEN

**THE GRILL DADS
(MARK ANDERSON & RYAN FEY)**

ALEX GUARNASCHELLI

ELIZABETH HEISKELL

CHING-HE HUANG

JJ JOHNSON

JUDY JOO

KATIE LEE BIEGEL

LAZARUS LYNCH

EDY MASSIH

HETTY MCKINNON

PRIYANKA NAIK

AYESHA NURDJAJA

KWAME ONWUACHI

ELIZABETH POETT

ALEJANDRA RAMOS

ADAM RICHMAN

ERIC RIPERT

JULIUS ROBERTS

ALISON ROMAN

DAVID ROSE

ALI ROSEN

MARCUS SAMUELSSON

STEFANO SECCHI

ALON SHAYA

NANCY SILVERTON

MICHAEL SOLOMONOV

HILLARY STERLING

MARTHA STEWART

CURTIS STONE

MICHAEL SYMON

JET TILA

CHRISTINA TOSI

ROZE TRAORE

LAURA VITALE

JERNARD WELLS

MOLLY YEH

"We check the rundown to see what's in the news, then we check the rundown for what we're going to eat that morning."

—Savannah Guthrie

INDEX

Produced and Written By:
Debbie Cohen Kosofsky, Emi Boscamp, and Katie Stilo

FOR ABRAMS
Editor: Holly Dolce
Designer: Danielle Youngsmith
Managing Editor: Lisa Silverman
Production Manager: Larry Pekarek

FOR THE TODAY SHOW
Writer: Emi Boscamp
Food Stylist/Recipe Developer: Katie Stilo
Senior Producer: Debbie Cohen Kosofsky
Project Manager: Savannah Smith

Library of Congress Control Number: 2024943705

ISBN: 978-1-4197-7820-9
eISBN: 979-8-88707-473-3

ABRAMS The Art of Books
195 Broadway, New York, NY 10007
abramsbooks.com